COLUMBIA RIVER GORGE

An Explorer's Guide

MIKE & KRISTY WESTBY

Majority of photos Copyright Mike Westby

Mosier Tunnel photo Copyright Ian Poellet

Cover photo © Brian Jannsen – www.BrianJannsen.com

Cover graphics by Sarah Craig – SarahCookDesign.com

Active, Oregon™

ISBN-13: 978-0998395067

10521 - CS

"Good roads are more than my hobby, they are my religion."

Sam Hill – Builder of the "King of Roads", the Columbia River Highway

FOLLOW
DISCOVER-OREGON

The Columbia River Gorge

On the Web:
www.Discover-Oregon.com

On Twitter:
@DiscoverOre.com

On Facebook:
www.Facebook.com/DiscoverORE

On Instagram:
DiscoverOregon4300

COLUMBIA RIVER GORGE –
AN EXPLORER'S GUIDE

The Columbia River Gorge is filled with an abundance of scenic and cultural riches. Dramatic overlooks offer endless views from atop towering basalt promontories, majestic stone amphitheatres cradle ever-flowing graceful waterfalls, and a ribbon of rich and ancient cultural history weaves its way through the gorge's entire length and beyond.

With *so many* destinations and attractions, how do you begin to discover what to see, do and explore when you visit the Gorge? The answer...the **Columbia River Gorge – An Explorer's Guide**. We've listed over 150 fun, exciting and fascinating attractions, destinations, and sites for you to visit, complete with descriptions, contact information, tips and usually a photo or two. Visit "Waterfall Alley", fly in a vintage bi-plane, cruise the "Fruit Loop", hike the Mosier Tunnels, fly along a zip line, dine at a fun café, see a giraffe, zebra or camel, eat the biggest ice cream cone of your life, walk among spring wildflowers, and enjoy countless panoramic vistas.

Enjoy exploring the Columbia River Gorge!

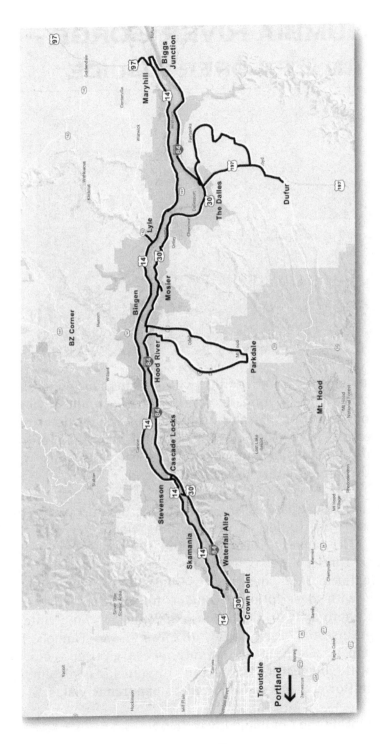

CONTENTS

Destinations

Troutdale, Crown Point & The
Historic Columbia River Highway 19

Columbia River Gorge Waterfalls 29

Bonneville Dam & Cascade Locks 39

Hood River 53

Mosier, The Dalles & Dufur 71

Maryhill, Schreiner Farms, Lyle & Bingen 97

Stevenson, Bonneville & Beacon Rock 117

Additional Information

Gorge Parking Permits 12

Helpful Phone Numbers 136

Visit Mt. Hood 144

The Historic Columbia River Highway 146

Average Monthly Fish Count Chart 148

How to Use This guide

Multnomah Falls - Columbia River Gorge

You may use this guide in two different ways...

Choose Your Columbia River Gorge Destination - Pick a destination, such as Cascade Locks, The Dalles, Hood River, Bingen, or the Historic Columbia River Highway, and then open this book to discover all of the sites you can visit at your destination for the day, weekend, or longer.

Or

Choose Your Columbia River Gorge Activity - Flip through the pages of the *Columbia River Gorge - An Explorer's Guide*, choose which activities you'd like to experience, and then venture forth! Want to tour the waterfalls of Waterfall Alley? Then head to Troutdale and make your way east along the Historic Columbia River Gorge Highway. Want to fly in a vintage bi-plane around Mt. Hood? Then you'll be looking to fly with TacAero out of Hood River. If you want to watch a stunning salmon masterpiece come to life from a plug of glass in a fiery furnace, then you're off to Nichol's Art Glass in The

Dalles. Or maybe you want to walk among fields of colorful wildflowers on a sunny spring day. If that's the case, then you'll be making your way to Catherine Creek, the Tom McCall Nature Preserve, or the Mosier Plateau. Find what excites your adventurous spirit and explore the Columbia River Gorge!

It's an Attractions Guide

While there are hundreds of hikes within the Columbia River Gorge, most of which we've enjoyed numerous times, this book is not a hiking guide, (though we do include some classics!) but instead reveals over 150 interesting attractions, sites and destinations within the Gorge. Inside these pages you'll find the Historic Columbia River Highway, the National Neon Sign Museum, an old-fashioned sternwheeler cruise, the first steam locomotive ever used in Oregon, an exciting zip line and aerial challenge course through the trees, over 300 antique automobiles and aeroplanes, ten graceful waterfalls, Oregon's oldest bookstore, some great new road cycling and mountain biking routes, an antique firefighting museum, nine historic hotels, places where you'll see bald eagles, hawks, owls, giraffes, zebras, camels, and a 10' sturgeon, the largest ice cream cone you'll ever eat in your life, and so much more!

The Historic Columbia River Highway

If you begin your journey through the Columbia River Gorge in Troutdale, you'll be traveling along the "King of Roads", the Historic Columbia River Highway. You will want to take a moment to read page 146 in this guide before you begin so as to learn more about this scenic Oregon icon and the amazing story behind it.

TIMING

A visit to the Columbia River Gorge is a beautiful trip most anytime of the year, with the conditions changing dramatically from season to season. Spring, summer and fall in "the Gorge" bring some of the finest weather in Oregon, as well as the entire United States, while winter can bring sunny mornings embraced by cool temperatures and wispy fog...or, quite often, treacherous icy conditions that can lock down travel for days. Be sure to check the weather forecast before setting out on your day of exploration.

WILDFLOWERS IN THE SPRINGTIME

If it is springtime and you like wildflowers, then you want to be in the gorge. Lupine, Chocolate Orchids, Penstemon, Indian Paintbrush, Howell's Daisy, Shooting Stars, Columbines and many others, including the dramatic Arrowleaf Balsamroot, cover the hillsides in an abundance of color. The wildflowers of the Columbia River Gorge do not bloom all at once, but instead over a period of about four months, usually mid-February through mid-June, with April and May offering the most vibrant displays. You'll find most of the wildflowers from the mid-gorge to points out east, with locations such as Rowena Crest, Catherine Creek (Page 110), Coyote Wall, the Dalles Mountain Ranch, the Mosier Plateau (Page 75) and many other sites offering outstanding experiences. While we list a couple of convenient wildflower spots in this guide, there are many more that are available with the aid of a short or long hike. If you are planning on visiting the gorge in the springtime, especially during April and May, we highly recommend you do an online search to learn more about the colorful Columbia River Gorge wildflowers.

THE COLORS OF AUTUMN

Every fall, the deciduous trees of the Columbia River Gorge paint a scene of striking fall colors. The hillsides become accented with yellows, oranges, and vibrant reds as the leaves of Birches, Aspens, Willows, Poplars, and Big Leaf Maples bid adieu to summer in a brilliant performance of autumn colors. It's Oregon's version of New England's fall colors, and you won't want to miss it if you are traveling here in late September and October.

POISON OAK
(& TICKS AND SNAKES)

"Leaves of three, let it be!"

Don't let this stop you from enjoying a hike during your visit, but be *very* mindful of poison oak when hiking in the Gorge, especially in the wooded areas at the eastern end. Just because you're having fun doesn't mean it's taking a break from what it does best, and that is to cause a very itchy, blistering rash. Its deep green leaves cluster in groups of three, and the plant itself typically grows up to a few feet off the ground, so be mindful of small children, as it is right at their height. Its shiny leaves can be tempting for a child to grasp, but that shine is the oil that causes the rash, so don't touch it or brush against it with your clothes. Note that symptoms of a rash can take 12 hours to 10 days to appear.

In addition to Poison Oak, keep an eye out for ticks, especially if you have a dog, as well as any snakes. Most are harmless, but the rocky terrain of the eastern Gorge can harbor rattlesnakes, and these are highly venomous.

COLUMBIA RIVER GORGE PARKING PERMITS

The Columbia River Gorge is bordered by the state of Washington on its northern side, and the state of Oregon on its southern side. Each state requires a parking permit for the use of their more popular State Parks, Trail Heads, Scenic Areas, etc. As a result, visitors will need an Oregon State Parks permit for visiting sites on the Oregon side of the Columbia River Gorge, and a Washington Parks Discover Pass for visiting sites on the Washington side. You may purchase two annual permits, one for each state, or you may purchase daily permits at the sites you choose to visit.

Oregon State Parks Day-Use Parking Permit – Daily: $5 – Annual: $30 – This permit is honored at all 26 Oregon State Parks that charge a parking fee. Permits are available at self-service kiosks, park booths, or offices located at the site in which a permit is required. In addition, they may be purchased by calling 800-551-6949 or online at https://www.oregonstateparks.org. Note that if you purchase a *daily* parking permit at one site in Oregon, you may use that permit at any other site in Oregon that requires the same permit *for the remainder of that day.* You do not need to buy a new permit at each site.

If you decide to hike any of the trails in the Gorge, note that 10 of the more popular trails require a parking pass, and this would need to be an Annual Northwest Forest Pass, a National Forest Recreation Day Pass, or an Interagency Annual, Senior or Access Pass.

Washington Parks Discover Pass - This permit is honored at over 100 Washington State Parks and recreation sites that charge a parking fee. Permits are available at self-service kiosks, licensed vendors, or offices located at the site in which a permit is required. In addition, they may be purchased by calling 866-320-9933 or online at https://www.discoverpass.wa.gov. Note that if you purchase a *daily* parking permit at one site in Washington, you may use that permit at any other site in Washington that requires the same permit *for the remainder of that day.* You do not need to buy a new permit at each site.

Online: https://www.discoverpass.wa.gov

- 1-Day Permit: $11.50
- Annual Permit: $35.00

At the Site:

- 1-Day Permit: $10.00 Cash
- Annual Permit: $30.00
  – Via credit card if a payment kiosk is available

Convenient Tip: Located in Troutdale, at the beginning of the Historic Columbia River Highway, is a Plaid Pantry store that sells annual (not daily) Oregon State Parks Day-Use Parking Permits, thus making it convenient to stop in here before beginning your exploration of the Gorge. Located right next to the large *Troutdale – Gateway to the Gorge* sign. (Page 20) Open 24 hours a day, 365 days per year. 246 W. Historic Columbia River Highway, Troutdale, OR 97060 – 503-665-8248

Bring Your Binoculars

 From dramatic waterfalls and distant volcanic peaks to circling hawks and soaring bald eagles, there is much to see when exploring the massive Columbia River Gorge, so you may want to consider tossing a good pair of binoculars in your daypack before heading out for the day.

Consider Some Good Paper Maps

We can't emphasize this enough. You will want to travel with and use good paper maps, and the more detailed, the better. Your phone will no doubt work well, but you're going to have the opportunity to explore some remote parts of the Columbia River Gorge, many of which have no cell signal, so your phone will not work there. In addition, paper maps will always boot up and never run out of power.

As you travel throughout the Gorge and stop at various locations, you'll often see folded Oregon maps made available for free by the Oregon Department of Transportation. These are very helpful, so grab more than one and keep them with you at all times. For more detail on the roads you'll be traveling, we also recommend the large Oregon atlases put out by DeLorme. You can find them online for about $25.

TAKE YOUR TIME
AND ENJOY THE SIGHTS

 As you make your way through this guide, you'll see a small clock icon placed next to some of the listings. There are many Gorge attractions that do not require much time to visit. A stop at the Vista House may require about half an hour, while a stop at Rowena Crest may require half that, but locations and attractions such as Multnomah Falls, the Bonneville Dam, the Mosier Tunnels, and the Maryhill Museum absolutely call for you to spend more time enjoying the commanding views or once-in-a-lifetime experiences. Wherever you see the clock icon, plan on spending at least an hour at that location, and we would encourage you to spend even more time there while hiking to a waterfall, exploring an interpretive center, sailing aboard a yacht, or even riding aboard a sternwheeler.

WHAT CAUSED THE FIRE?

As you make your way along the western end of the Historic Columbia River Highway, you'll notice obvious signs of a large fire that swept through the area, as evidenced by swaths of trees with blackened trunks, chainsawed stumps, and silver tree snags covering nearby hillsides and distant ridges.

In September of 2017, a teenage boy carelessly tossed a lit firework into dry grass and leaves while hiking in the Columbia River Gorge and set off a massive wildfire that burned for weeks, closed I-84 for an extended period, forced the evacuation of hundreds of people from their homes, destroyed many historic trails and structures in the Gorge, and consumed nearly 50,000 acres of forest land. Thankfully, only 15% of that area was rated as "Highly Burned".

Thanks to the brave efforts of hardworking firefighters and emergency responders, as well as countless volunteers and the citizens of communities throughout the Columbia River Gorge, most of the Gorge was saved from this devastating wildfire, and today trails are being reopened, bridges are being rebuilt, and the burned areas are again springing to back life.

DUCK, DUCK, GORGE!

Every year, well over 4,000,000 vehicle trips occur through the Columbia River Gorge. Hikers, bikers, skiers, cyclists, sailboarders, semi-truck drivers, college students on their way to school, even folks just making their way to grandma and grandpa's house ply the I-84 Interstate. However, only a very, very small percentage of these drivers ever notice a fun bit of whimsy hidden in the trees right next to their drive. Secretly tucked high in the branches of two trees found at different locations along the interstate are a couple of large duck decoys. Clearly out of their element, one can be found sitting on a branch approximately 20' up in a tree, (photo) while another is more than 30' high! Placed here by mischievous pranksters or perhaps some ODOT workers who are in charge of keeping the trees trimmed, the duck decoys vigilantly keep watch over 12,000 cars that pass below every day.

So where are these two whimsical ducks? Go ahead and send us an email at ContactUs@Discover-Oregon.com and we'll let you know exactly where you can find them. Have you happened to discover even more decoys, or do you know the story behind these two? Then get in touch with us and let us know, and we'll include the story in an upcoming edition of this guide.

Note: If you do spot the duck decoys, DO NOT pull over and take a photo of them. If people begin stopping and taking photos, then ODOT will definitely remove them, since they will have become a roadway hazard.

YO, NO QUID PRO QUO

As you use this guide, you'll notice that we mention a number of different restaurants, coffee shops, hotels, museums, attractions, and other retail destinations all throughout the guide itself and in its back pages. We'd like you to know that none of these destinations have paid to be included within our guide, nor provided us with any form of compensation. We have included them only because we thought you'd like to know about them, they add to the Columbia River Gorge experience, and we're big fans of small businesses and the entrepreneurial spirit.

BLACK & WHITE PHOTOS

So, what's up with the black and white photos instead of color? Well, we'd *really* like to use color photos throughout our guide. Seriously, that would be great! However, in order to reach economies of scale and keep the book affordable if we were to use color photos, we'd have to print thousands of copies at a time and probably store them on pallets in our garage. That's all well and fine, but it would mean that we couldn't make any updates to this guidebook until all of those copies were sold, which would take years. In order to regularly make updates, add new destinations, include more information, and even add additional photos, we use print-on-demand technology to print much smaller runs of books at a time. The only downside is that if we were to use color photos with POD technology, the costs involved with using color with these smaller print runs would make this guidebook prohibitively expensive, so the compromise is...black and white photos.

TROUTDALE,
CROWN POINT VISTA HOUSE &
THE HISTORIC COLUMBIA
RIVER HIGHWAY

TROUTDALE

Troutdale, OR represents the western "Gateway to the Gorge." Here, visitors can stop in at the small shops and boutiques, visit a museum or two, or grab a bite to eat before spending the day exploring the Gorge. Troutdale is also a great place to begin your travels on the Historic Columbia River Gorge Highway as it makes its way east along "Waterfall Alley".

To reach Troutdale...

- Travel I-84 East and take Exit 17.

- Continue straight from the exit for 0.7 mile to Graham Road. Turn right here and follow this south for 0.3 mile to the Columbia River Highway / Historic Route 30. Turn left / east here, where you'll then pass under the large "Gateway to the Gorge" sign.

- You are now on the Historic Columbia River Highway Scenic Byway, which leads to the Barn Exhibit Hall, The Women's Forum Overlook, Crown Point Vista House, Waterfall Alley, Multnomah Falls and out into the Columbia River Gorge.

www.Discover-Oregon.com

Rail Depot Museum - Depot Park

Railroads have played a very important role in shaping the history of the gorge, as their influence here reaches all the way back to the mid-1800s. In fact, the very first steam locomotive ever used in the Oregon Territory, The Oregon Pony, plied its tracks in  Cascade Locks, where it you can find it today, and in Troutdale, you'll find the Troutdale Rail Depot Museum. Originally built in 1882 and rebuilt in 1907 after it burned, the museum offers visitors a look at just how the depot appeared when it was in use in the early 1900s. In addition, rail fans will find a nicely restored Union Pacific caboose in the parking lot.

Rail Depot Museum
473 E. Historic Columbia River Highway
Troutdale, OR 97060
503-661-2164

- Open: Every Friday from 10:00 a.m. to 2:00 p.m.

 Harlow House Museum & Park

 Built in 1900, the Harlow House showcases the lifestyle, furnishings and belongings of families in the area at the turn of the 20th century. In addition, visitors will find changing exhibits, photos, artwork, and a short interpretive pathway outside.

Harlow House Museum & Park
762 E. Historic Columbia River Highway
Troutdale, OR 97060
503-661-2164

- Open: Sunday – 1:00 p.m. to 3:00 p.m.

 ## Barn Exhibit Hall

The large Barn Exhibit Hall features changing exhibits which tell of the rich history of Troutdale and the surrounding area. Currently, visitors will find an impressively curated exhibit marking the 100th anniversary of the Historic Columbia River Highway, the first highway in the United States to be built as a scenic road, as well as the first to include a painted center line. If you're interested in learning about the history of the Historic Columbia River Highway, this is *the* place to visit.

Barn Exhibit Hall
732 E. Historic Columbia River Highway
Troutdale, OR 97060
503-661-2164

- Open: Wednesday through Saturday – 10:00 a.m. to 3:00 p.m., Sunday – 1:00 p.m. to 3:00 p.m.

 ## Sugarpine Drive In

Located in a former 1920 gas station at the beginning of the Historic Columbia River Highway, the Sugarpine Drive In is perfect for a snack or meal before you head out to explore the Columbia River Gorge, or perhaps a large chocolate and vanilla swirl sundae afterwards! However, don't expect greasy fare at this drive-in, but instead savor their gourmet offerings featuring fresh top quality locally sourced ingredients.

Sugarpine Drive In
1208 E Historic Columbia River Highway
Troutdale, OR 97060
503-665-6558

- Open: Thursday through Monday – 11:00 a.m. to 7:00 p.m.

 ## Womans Forum Overlook

 From 1912 to 1930, this spot was home to the Chanticleer Inn. Known for its famous chicken dinners, it was *the* place for the Portland elite to gather when setting out on an adventure beyond Portland. However, getting here was quite the chore, as travelers would have to journey 25 miles by train or boat to the base of the cliff below and then walk or shuttle by horse-drawn wagon up a steep dirt road to the inn. (You can find remnants of the old road as it disappears into the woods at the north end of the parking lot) Like so many buildings of this era, the Chanticleer Inn burned down, on October 8th, 1930. (Photo Circa 1916)

Today, the Women's Forum Overlook is a tribute to the founding members of the Portland Women's Forum, who worked tirelessly to raise the funds necessary to buy this point and preserve its amazing view for future generations.

The Women's Forum Overlook is located a little over one mile west of the Crown Point Vista House, on the Historic Columbia River Highway.

 Larch Mountain Summit Viewpoint / Sherrard Point. 🌲

Throughout the Gorge, you'll find a wealth of panoramic vistas from impressive viewpoints. Larch Mountain Summit, however, provides a "reach out and touch it" view of majestic Mt. Hood over a sea of towering fir trees, as well as views of Mt. Rainier,  Mt. St. Helens, Mt. Adams and in the far distance, Mt. Jefferson. It's a captivating spectacle anytime of the year, but especially in the spring when the mountains are blanketed in deep snow.

To drive to the summit of Larch Mountain, turn onto East Larch Mountain Road, which you'll find approximately 0.7 miles west of the Crown Point Vista House, and follow this for 14 miles to a large paved parking area. Park here and take the nearby paved path and long set of stairs that lead to a fenced in viewpoint. Note that East Larch Mountain Road is closed with a gate 10 miles up the road from late fall to early spring. It is also a popular road with cyclists, so be sure to keep a careful eye out for them as you drive to the summit and back.

CROWN POINT VISTA HOUSE

Offering a commanding view into the heart of the Columbia River Gorge at the west end of the old Columbia River Highway, the Crown Point Vista House is one of Oregon's classic historical icons. Built atop a massive basalt promontory in 1917, its  unique stone structure is "a temple to the natural beauty of the Gorge." Inside, travelers will find a museum showcasing the history of the building and the Columbia River Gorge, as well as a small gift shop, restrooms, and a café serving coffee.

Crown Point Vista House
40700 E. Columbia River Highway
Corbett, OR 97019
503-344-1368

* Open Daily: 9:00 a.m. – 4:00 p.m.
* Closed if winds exceed 50 mph or if conditions are snowy or icy.

 Bridal Veil Post Office

It may be tiny at 110 square feet, and not many people visit it, but its still one of the most popular destinations in the Columbia River Gorge. Every year, the historical Bridal Veil Post Office, the third smallest in the country, processes over 190,000 pieces of mail from  brides all around the world as they seek to have their wedding invitations stamped with the romantic Bridal Veil postmark and the image of two interlocking hearts or doves.

Bridal Veil Post Office
47100 W Mill Road
Bridal Veil, OR 97010
800-275-8777

- Open: Monday through Friday - 11:30 a.m. to 3:30 p.m., Saturday - 9:30 a.m. to 3:30 p.m., Closed on Sunday

 ## Bridal Veil Cemetery

Take the unmarked narrow dirt road off of the Historic Columbia River Highway and find one of the two remaining elements of the historical town of Bridal Veil, the small and well-tended Bridal Veil Cemetery. (The other being the Bridal Veil Post Office) Here, you'll find 43 tombstones honoring early pioneers of the area, with the first being laid to rest in the year 1888.

Bridal Veil Cemetery
47910 E Crown Point Hwy
Corbett, OR 97019

Note that the dirt road to the cemetery angles sharply and slightly downward to the north off of the Historic Columbia River Highway. It looks a lot like a driveway, and that's because it is. You're welcome to follow the road to the cemetery and park in one of the two spaces available, but do not continue to the home next door.

Simon Benson Bridge – Multnomah Falls

COLUMBIA RIVER GORGE
WATERFALLS

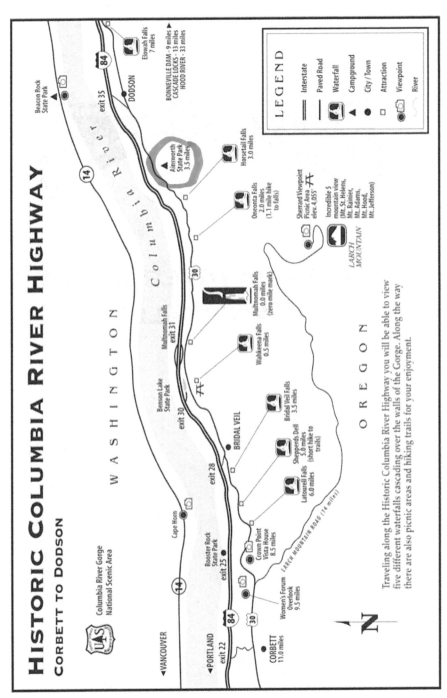

HISTORIC COLUMBIA RIVER HIGHWAY

CORBETT TO DODSON

Columbia River Gorge
National Scenic Area

Traveling along the Historic Columbia River Highway you will be able to view five different waterfalls cascading over the walls of the Gorge. Along the way there are also picnic areas and hiking trails for your enjoyment.

LEGEND
- Interstate
- Paved Road
- Waterfall
- Campground
- City / Town
- Attraction
- Viewpoint
- River

Beacon Rock State Park

WASHINGTON

Columbia River

OREGON

◄VANCOUVER

◄PORTLAND

CORBETT
exit 22
11.0 miles

Women's Forum Overlook
9.5 miles

Crown Point Vista House
8.5 miles

Rooster Rock State Park
exit 25

Cape Horn

Latourell Falls
6.0 miles

Sheppards Dell
5.0 miles
(short hike to trails)

Bridal Veil Falls
3.5 miles

BRIDAL VEIL

Benson Lake State Park
exit 30

Wahkeena Falls
0.5 miles

Multnomah Falls
exit 31

Multnomah Falls
0.0 miles
(zero mile mark)

LARCH MOUNTAIN ROAD (14 miles)

LARCH MOUNTAIN

Sherrard Viewpoint Picnic Area
elev. 4,055'

Incredible 5 mountain view
(Mt. St. Helens, Mt. Rainier, Mt. Adams, Mt. Hood, Mt. Jefferson)

Oneonta Falls
2.0 miles
(1.1 mile hike to falls)

Ainsworth State Park
3.5 miles

Horsetail Falls
3.0 miles

DODSON
exit 35

Elowah Falls
7 miles

BONNEVILLE DAM - 9 miles
CASCADE LOCKS - 13 miles
HOOD RIVER - 33 miles

N

Map courtesy of Friends of Multnomah Falls

COLUMBIA RIVER GORGE WATERFALLS

The Columbia River Gorge is home to over two dozen beautiful waterfalls close to the highway, with Multnomah Falls being by far the most popular. Appearing one after the other as you motor along, stop and visit any one of them along this stretch of the Historic Columbia River Highway. Many, such as Latourell Falls, offer short hikes with a very rewarding view.

Appearing in order as you drive east from the Crown Point Vista House:

- Latourell Falls
- Shepperd's Dell
- Bridal Veil Falls
- Wahkeena Falls
- Multnomah Falls
- Oneonta Falls
- Horsetail Falls
- Elowah Falls

Note: Car break-ins along this stretch of the Columbia River Gorge are a chronic problem. If you stop to admire the waterfalls and enjoy some of the short hikes, DO NOT leave valuables inside your car, nor leave bags which appear tempting within sight. Yes, you know there's nothing in that backpack, but thieves found a wallet in the last one they stole, so they'll take yours just to see what's inside. In addition, do not arrive, get out and put valuables, such as a purse or a pack, into your trunk and walk away. There is a history of thieves watching for this kind of activity so as to learn what you have and where it is stored. Because of its quick access to I-84, break-ins occur throughout this area, but especially in the Multnomah Falls and Oneonta Gorge parking lots.

Bridal Veil Falls Photo © Megan Westby

 ## Latourell Falls

 Introduce yourself to the waterfalls of the Columbia River Gorge with beautiful Latourell Falls. Featuring a large amphitheatre with striking columnar basalt and a distinct yellow patch of lichen, Latourell Falls drops uninterrupted for 224 feet, often in a thin stream, before disappearing into a pool below. Follow the stairs from the parking lot, which take you up to a trail that leads to a viewpoint only a short distance away, or opt to take a slightly descending path from the west side of the parking area, near the road, to the base of the falls. Once there, cross a small foot bridge and follow the paved path only a short distance further to see an amazing example of the Arch Deck Bridge design employed by Sam Hill and Samuel Lancaster when building the Historic Columbia River Highway.

Shepperd's Dell Falls

Named after George Shepperd, the land owner who presented the falls and its accompanying 11 acre parcel to the City of Portland in May of 1915, Shepperd's Dell Falls drops over 90 feet in a two-tiered display before making its way under a classic 1914 deck arch bridge, a captivating example of the impressive engineering employed with the Historic Columbia River Highway. Find the beginning of the short paved path to the falls down a small flight of stairs, near the east end of the bridge.

Bridal Veil Falls

You have your choice of two paths at Bridal Veil Falls. One leads to sweeping vistas of the Columbia River Gorge, while the other takes you to a viewing platform opposite the falls.

Make your way to the east end of the parking lot and find a trail that splits near the restrooms. The paved path to the left takes you on a short interpretive loop which leads to a collection of viewpoints high on a bluff overlooking the Columbia River. Choose the path that veers to the right, and you'll soon drop down into the forest along a gravel path that traverses a set of switchbacks, small bridges and concrete steps before leading up to a viewing platform across from Bridal Veil Falls. It's about ¼ mile, at best. Note that you'll want to be mindful of the poison oak in this area.

Wahkeena Falls

A short 0.2 mile hike along a paved path takes you up to a historic hand-crafted stone bridge fronting Wahkeena Falls. Dropping as a fall and then a cascade for over 240 feet, it is one of the more photogenic falls you'll find in the Columbia River Gorge.

Multnomah Falls

Falling in two stages, separated by the historic Benson Bridge, Multnomah Falls towers at 620 feet high, making it the tallest waterfall in all of Oregon and creating such an impressive site that it draws more than 2 million visitors every year. In fact, it is the most visited natural recreation site in the Pacific Northwest.

The walk from the often busy parking area to the falls is very short, and the option exists to hike a trail up to the Benson Bridge or to continue on all the way up to a viewing platform at the crest of the upper falls for a unique and memorable view. (1.2 Miles)

Multnomah Falls Lodge, built in 1925, offers a Visitor Center, gift shop, a snack bar, and a restaurant which serves breakfast at 8:00 a.m., lunch at 11:00 a.m., and dinner at 4:00 p.m.

- Open: Multnomah Falls is open year-round, and the Visitor Center is open daily from 9:00 a.m. to 5:00 p.m.

After visiting Multnomah Falls, you'll continue to Oneonta Falls, Horsetail Falls, and Elowah Falls. To do so, travel east from Multnomah Falls on the Historic Columbia River Scenic Byway for 3.6 miles to where you take the road to the right for *Hood River – I-84 – Route 30 East.* Take this and continue a little more than 0.2 miles to where you turn right onto Frontage Road *instead of taking the onramp to I-84 Eastbound on the left.* Continue on Frontage Road until you come to the trailhead for Elowah Falls.

Oneonta Falls

A unique Columbia River Gorge adventure. In addition to offering hiking trails to Lower, Middle, and Upper Oneonta Falls, visitors may also climb over a large log jam and wade through Oneonta Creek up Oneonta Canyon to the base of Oneonta Falls. It's a popular hike, though most folks wait until the water level is low, since the water can be a tad cool!

Note: Due to the fire of 2017, all of the trails to Oneonta Falls, including through Oneonta Creek, are closed for an indefinite period of time.

Horsetail Falls

Located right next to the Historic Columbia River Highway, graceful Horsetail Falls drops as a flowing ribbon for a full 176 feet before dispersing into a large pool at its base. Park and walk across the highway to a nearby observation area at the base of the falls.

Elowah Falls

Plunging over a dramatic cliff face and free-falling for over 200 feet, Elowah Falls rewards those who make the easy 0.8 mile hike to its base with a captivating picturesque scene. A striking basalt amphitheatre offering scattered patches of bright yellow and green lichen forms the backdrop as the water falls and disperses below before disappearing amidst mossy boulders as McCord Creek.

Note: Due to the fire of 2017, the trail to Elowah Falls will be closed for safety reasons for an indefinite period.

 ## Historic Columbia River Highway State Trail – Elowah Falls to Cascade Locks

The parking lot for Elowah Falls (The John B. Yeon Trailhead) is an excellent spot at which to jump onto a section of the Historic Columbia River Highway *State Trail* that leads a little over six miles from this portion of the Historic Columbia River Highway to Cascade Locks and beyond. Note that the trail is paved and open to cyclists and pedestrians on foot.

Columbia Gorge Sternwheeler

BONNEVILLE DAM
& CASCADE LOCKS

BONNEVILLE LOCK & DAM

As you make your way deep into the Columbia River Gorge, you'll find yourself at the Bonneville Lock & Dam. (I-84 Exit 40) Built in 1934 by the US Corps of Engineers with funding from the Works Progress Administration, the dam provided thousands of jobs for those who were out of work because of the depression. Today, in addition to providing safe passage for river vessels, it captures the mighty Columbia and harnesses its power for use in a myriad ways throughout the Pacific Northwest.

The Locks at the Bonneville Dam

It's not everyday that you get to see vessels large and small up close as they pass through a large river lock...well, unless you work at the locks of Bonneville Dam! On your way to visiting the Bonneville Lock & Dam Visitor Center, take the first right after passing through the guard shack, park, and then walk over to the railing to get a sense of vertigo as you peer into the locks holding back the river with their massive gates. Hopefully, your timing will be good and a ship will be passing through while you're there. If not, don't bother asking when one will be arriving next, as the lock tenders do not have any of that information. When a ship shows up, they simply work the gates to allow it to pass before waiting for the next ship to appear.

Bonneville Dam Fish Viewing Window / Bonneville Lock & Dam Visitor Center

This is either a unique taste of Oregon that provides an up close look at the migrating salmon of the Columbia River, combined with an interesting lesson on the building of the Bonneville Dam...or it's a dose of disappointment mixed with history.

A view into the fish ladder

Much of this experience depends upon if the salmon are running or not, so it's best to call the interpretive center or the Fish Count Hotline beforehand to ask if any salmon are currently migrating upriver past the viewing window. Fish runs in the spring, as well as late August through October, peaking in September, provide plenty of fish to see.

- Also see the *Average Monthly Fish Count Chart* on page 148 to see if fish may be running during your visit.
- Bonneville Dam Interpretive Center: 541-374-8820
- Fish Count Hotline: 541-374-4011

Driving Directions: Take Exit 40 from I-84 – Turn north at the stop and proceed under I-84 onto NE Bonneville Way. Stop at the armed security checkpoint and then proceed across the locks to the large parking lot on the east side of the interpretive center. Directions to the Fish Viewing Window are clearly displayed inside the interpretive center.

Bonneville Dam Hatchery

Open to the public year-round, the Bonneville Hatchery at the Bonneville Lock & Dam has display ponds holding thousands of trout and salmon fry, as well as sturgeon. Make your way to the small Sturgeon Viewing and Interpretive Center behind the hatchery  building and step inside to see *huge* sturgeon and salmon swimming past the large viewing window. It is here that you'll see Herman, an adult White Sturgeon measuring more than 10' in length! Also, be sure to see the nearby Trout Pond, where the 18" trout are small in comparison to the others. Be sure to have a quarter in hand so you can buy food to feed the fish!

Bonneville Dam Hatchery
70543 NE Herman Loop
Cascade Locks, OR 97014
541-374-8393

- Exit 40 – I-84
- Located west of the
  Bonneville Dam

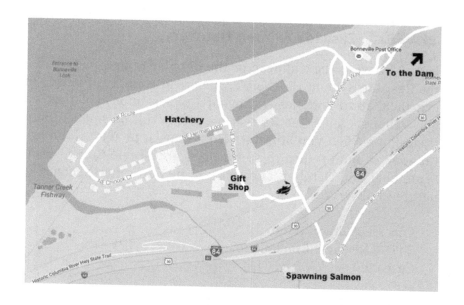

Driving Directions: Take Exit 40 from I-84 and turn north to proceed under I-84 onto NE Bonneville Way. In a short distance, turn left onto NE Sturgeon Ln. and park near the gift shop. Then walk over to the hatchery.

If you are coming here from the Bonneville Dam Fish Viewing Window, (Page 41) look for signs to the hatchery / NE Sturgeon Ln. as you begin to leave the Dam area and approach I-84.

Spawning Salmon (Sept. & Oct.)

During the last days of August, as well as the months of September and October, visitors to the Bonneville Lock & Dam area can see spawning salmon in nearby Tanner Creek.

Driving Directions: Exit I-84 at Exit 40, but instead of turning left and passing under I-84 to Bonneville Dam, turn right and park at the Wahclella Falls trailhead. (Which is an excellent two mile round trip triple-falls hike, by the way.) Walk over to the nearby Tanner Creek to see the salmon. Note that a parking permit, such as a Northwest Forest Pass, is required here.

43

Cascade Salmon Hatchery

Located next to the trailhead of the popular Eagle Creek Trail is the Cascade Salmon Hatchery. Open year-round, it focuses on egg incubation and the rearing of Coho salmon, so there's a good chance you'll see its rearing ponds full of small salmon fingerlings when you stop by. Note that large adult Coho and Chinook salmon return to spawn in nearby Eagle Creek during September and October, and this can be quite the spectacle of nature to observe.

Cascade Salmon Hatchery
74152 NE Eagle Creek Loop
Cascade Locks, OR 97014

- Open: 7:30 a.m. to 4:30 p.m., though visitors can walk around the rearing ponds after hours. Personnel are more than happy to answer any questions visitors may have while the facility is open.

Note: A parking permit is not needed when parking at the hatchery. However, if you park near the busy Eagle Creek Trail trailhead just to the south, then you will need an Annual Northwest Forest Pass, a National Forest Recreation Day Pass, or an Interagency Annual, Senior or Access Pass.

 ## Eagle Creek Overlook

 Built in 1937 by the Civilian Conservation Corp, the Eagle Creek Overlook gave sightseers a place from which to watch the construction of the massive Bonneville Dam. Today, it gives travelers a captivating view of the dam and the river that's a little bit off the beaten path and well worth the stop.

Driving Directions: From the Cascade Hatchery, follow the narrow road that winds west between Eagle Creek and I-84, before turning north to pass under I-84. Park in the parking area for the Eagle Creek Overlook and follow the short trail at the north end of the parking area as it makes its way up a couple of switchbacks with stairs to the overlook.

Note that the stretch of Eagle Creek next to the road leading west is an excellent spot to see migrating salmon during September and October.

CASCADE LOCKS

Located in the heart of the Columbia River Gorge at Exit 44, the town of Cascade Locks welcomes visitors with a growing number of restaurants, a wealth of adventure, and a fascinating story that reveals the history of the indigenous people of the area, the courage of the Oregon Trail pioneers, and the powerful forces that shaped the gorge.

 Cascade Locks Historical Museum

Built in 1905, the museum provides guests with a look at the history of the Cascade Locks area through displays, photos and artifacts. Outside, in its own climate controlled building, is The Oregon Pony, the first steam locomotive ever used in Oregon.

Cascade Locks Historical Museum
SW Portage Rd.
Cascade Locks, OR 97014

- Open May – September - 12:00 p.m. – 5:00 p.m. - $4
- Closed Mondays, except holidays

Thunder Island

Take a moment to walk across the locks, which were built in 1896, and explore the park-like setting of Thunder Island. It's an excellent way to see the locks up close, and the far shore of the island provides a beautiful view of the river, as well as a great place to enjoy a scenic lunch.

Walking Directions: Walk north to the foot bridge located just north of the Cascade Locks Historical Museum and cross over the locks to Thunder Island.

Set Sail on the Columbia River

One of our favorite things to do is enjoy a picnic on Thunder Island while overlooking the flowing Columbia River, but even better is a sailing adventure out on the river itself! It's easy to do...simply make a reservation *at least* two hours in advance via online or by calling, drive out to Cascade Locks and meet your hosts, Preston and Chennie, and then board their beautiful 38' sloop "Wy'East" for a two hour sailing adventure. Choose to help sail the boat or just sit back and enjoy the view. Sunset sails are also available and they are especially beautiful in this part of the gorge. By the way, the boat is a unique and very memorable wedding venue, as well.

Note that Wy'East holds two to six passengers. Visit their web site for additional details and to make a reservation.

Heart of the Gorge Sailing
Cascade Locks Marina
Cascade Locks, OR 97014
941-400-0050
Email: HeartoftheGorgeSailing@gmail.com
www.HeartoftheGorgeSailing.com

 ## Columbia Gorge Sternwheeler Cruise

See the Columbia River Gorge from "the best view on the Columbia" during a one or two hour sightseeing and interpretive cruise aboard the historic Columbia Gorge Sternwheeler. Approximately three cruises per day in the summer. Call 503-224-3900 to book your cruise.

Columbia Gorge Sternwheeler
299 SW Portage Rd.
Cascade Locks, OR 97014
541-374-8427

Note that the **Locks Waterfront Café**, where you board the sternwheeler, is a fine place to have lunch, especially outside on a nice summer day when you can watch the sternwheeler arrive and depart. It is open from 10:30 a.m. – 6:00 p.m. daily, May to October. 541-645-0372

 ## Sacagawea Statue

See this beautiful larger-than-life bronze statue of Sacagawea, (Sah-cog-a-way) as well as Captain Meriwether Lewis' Newfoundland dog Seaman, located outside the Visitor Center and Locks Waterfront Cafe at 299 SW Portage Rd., Cascade Locks.

Train Appreciation Park

Life is better with a bit of whimsy, and you'll find some on the corner of NW Forest Ln. and Shahala Drive. Here, a single bench sits at the back of a grassy corner overlooking a bus stop and a set of railroad tracks a short distance away. Add a sign overhead and you have the simple yet whimsical "Train Appreciation Park." Take a seat, wait for a train to pass...and appreciate it!

Directions: From Wa Na Pa Street, turn northeast onto Forest Ln. and follow this 1.3 miles to the park, which you'll find on the south side of the street.

Hike & Bike the Easy Climb Trail

Even if you've been to the Columbia River Gorge many times, this short hike reveals an all new perspective of the river as it takes visitors along part of the Easy Climb mountain bike trail to different vantage points situated atop vertical cliffs high above the water's edge.

If you're new to mountain biking or would like to give it a try for the first time, then you'll like the Easy Climb Trail, as it was purposely designed for beginners. Meandering through tall White Oaks and open grasslands, the 3 mile trail contains less than 200 feet of elevation gain, so it's perfect for getting a sense of how to handle your mountain bike on single track with little in the way of challenging terrain. The trail is open to biking and hiking

only, and you'll want to keep an eye out for poison oak.

Driving Directions: From Wa Na Pa Street, (The main road through Cascade Locks) "Y" left onto Forest Ln. at the east end of town. In 1.8 miles, turn left / north onto Industrial Park Way and continue for another .5 mile to a large gravel parking area on the right. Park at the sign for the Easy Climb trailhead.

Eastwind Drive-In

The place to hit after a day of adventure in the Columbia River Gorge, the Eastwind Drive-In offers burgers, fries, shakes and the largest chocolate & vanilla swirl soft-serve ice cream cone you'll ever see in your life! Simply continue down the main drag of Cascade Locks after getting off I-84, and you'll see it on the north side of the road.

Eastwind Drive-In
395 NW Wa Na Pa Street
Cascade Locks, OR 97014
541-374-8380

Brigham Fish Market

If the day calls for some delicious seafood, including halibut, shrimp, clams, and oysters, as well as freshly caught Columbia River salmon and sturgeon, all prepared in a variety of ways, including Gluten Free, then stop in at one of our favorite Cascade Locks restaurants, Brigham Fish Market. Grab a table inside or enjoy outdoor seating in the sun. (Be sure to try the smoked steelhead!)

49

Brigham Fish Market
681 Wa Na Pa Street
Cascade Locks, OR 97014
541-374-9340

Open:

- Monday and Tuesday – 11:00 a.m. to 6:00 p.m.
- Thursday through Sunday – 10:00 a.m. to 6:00 p.m.
- Closed Wednesdays

Thirsty Coffee Bar

Want to find your new favorite spot to grab a flavorful coffee, hot chocolate, iced tea, smoothie, breakfast sandwich, pastry or more when exploring the gorge? Then stop in at Thirsty Coffee Bar and enjoy their locally made offerings. Oh, and be sure to ask about The Joy Foundation.

Thirsty Coffee Bar
504 Wa Na Pa Street
Cascade Locks, OR 97014

- Open Monday through Saturday – 6:00 a.m. to 6:00 p.m., Sundays – 7:00 a.m. to 6:00 p.m.

Bridgeside Restaurant

Located right next to the dramatic Bridge of the Gods, this historic family restaurant opens early and is a favorite stop for locals, Pacific Crest Trail through hikers, and Columbia River Gorge explorers of all ages who enjoy its home-style cooking served

with commanding views of the Columbia River below.

Bridgeside Restaurant
745 NW Wa Na Pa Street
Cascade Locks, OR 97014

- Hours: Daily – 6:30 a.m. to 9:00 p.m.

Thunder Island Brewing Company

Thunder Island Brewing Co. offers a large selection of In-House Beers, as well as regional favorites, local wines, ciders, teas, and soft drinks. Of course, a good beer needs a good meal, and you'll find a nice selection of American fare, including salads, burgers,

sandwiches, ribs, sea salted fries, and more, all in their new restaurant. *Photo credit: Jessica Hill*

Thunder Island Brewing Co.
601 NW Wa Na Pa St.
Cascade Locks, OR 97014

- Hours: Summer: Daily – 11:00 a.m. to 9:00 p.m.
- Winter: Sunday through Thurs – 12:00 p.m. to 8:00 p.m., Friday & Saturday – 11:00 a.m. to 9:00 p.m.

HOOD RIVER

HOOD RIVER

Home to a busy downtown area filled with recreation-minded folks, the town of Hood River is a launching point for countless outdoor adventures on the eastern end of the Columbia River Gorge National Scenic Area. Explore an amazing collection of antique planes and automobiles, take to the skies in a historic biplane, walk and shop in "old town" Hood River, enjoy some hand-dipped huckleberry ice cream, travel the famous Hood River Fruit Loop, step into history at a museum or two, watch some world-class sailboarding up close, and taste your new favorite wine for the very first time. (I-84 - Exits 62, 63 & 64)

 Historic Broughton Flume

As you begin to approach Hood River on I-84 from the west, you'll see a large freeway sign on the right which reads *Exit 58 – Mitchell Point Overlook.* Do not take this exit, but at this point, while you're driving, look directly ahead to the opposite shore of the  Columbia River and you'll spot a gray horizontal ribbon of old timbers and planks crossing a talus field of rocks just above the river. These boards are the remains of the historic Broughton Flume, a raised wooden flume, or channel of water, which carried rough-cut lumber down a fast moving water stream for nine miles from a sawmill in Willard, WA to the old Broughton Mill at Hood, WA, on the bank of the Columbia River. With a 1,000' drop along the way, the lumber moved quickly, thus making the flume an efficient means by which to move the rough-cut lumber to the mill, where it was then processed and recut into finished lumber before being shipped out on the Spokane, Portland & Seattle Railway, (SP&S) which ran in this section of the Gorge until 1956.

The Broughton Flume, which was the longest and fastest water flume in the world, was in operation from 1923 to 1986, when it was abandoned. Today, you can still see fading ribbons of the old flume, and sections have been preserved in Willard, WA and at the Columbia Gorge Interpretive Center in Stevenson, Washington. *Historical photo courtesy of the History Museum of Hood River County.*

 ### Egg River Cafe

Whether you're stopping for breakfast or lunch, you'll enjoy the Egg River Café, just as all the locals do. An extensive menu offers your favorite breakfast items, all made with fresh local ingredients. Enjoy large portions of home-made pancakes and waffles, Egg River skillets, mixed scrambles, breakfast burritos, and even pancake, French toast or waffle sandwiches!

Egg River Café
1313 Oak Street
Hood River, OR 97031
541-386-1127

- Open: Daily – 6:00 a.m. to 2:00 p.m.

Note that there is parking for the Egg River Café in the small parking lot across the street, and the peak you see in the far distance here is 12,280' Mt. Adams.

Bette's Place

If the wait is too long at the Egg River Café, then head down the road a little ways to the "Friendliest Restaurant in Town", Bette's Place. Here you'll find a full menu of breakfast fare, as well as grandma's warm cinnamon rolls.

Bette's Place
416 Oak Street
Hood River, OR 97031
541-386-1880

- Open: Daily – 5:30 a.m. to 3:00 p.m.

 Mike's Ice Cream

If you're in the mood for some delicious hand-scooped ice cream, then Mike's Ice Cream is the place to go. Stop in after spending the day exploring the Hood River Valley, Mosier Tunnels Trail, or the eastern end of the Columbia River Gorge. It's always busy when it's warm out, so order a double scoop, grab a chair, and join in the fun. *Note that Mike's accepts only cash or checks.*

Mike's Ice Cream
504 Oak Street
Hood River, OR 97031
541-386-6260

- Open: Daily - April 1 to October 31 – Summer: 11:00 a.m. to 11:00 p.m. – Spring and Fall: Noon-ish to 8:00 p.m....maybe 9:00 p.m. if the day calls for it.

Explore Hood River Shops

Oak Street in old town Hood River is home to a collection of interesting shops, stores, boutiques and more. Take some time this morning to walk the street and pop into various shops to see what you just can't live without. Along the way, you'll find bookstores, boutiques, gift shops, a surf shop, bicycle shops, sports shops, a hobby shop, a shop for your dog, and a kids shop named G Willikers Toy Shoppe. That's a lot of shops!

Western Antique Aeroplane & Automobile Museum (WAAAM)

Stroll among an amazing collection of over 130 flight-ready antique aeroplanes, along with over 180 intricately restored automobiles from the 1910s through 1950s, all under two large hangars spanning over 3.5 acres. In addition, visitors will find antique tractors, motorcycles, military vehicles, toys and more.

Western Antique Aeroplane & Automobile Museum
1600 Air Museum Rd.
Hood River, OR 97031
541-308-1600

- Open Daily 9:00 a.m. – 5:00 p.m. – Closed Thanksgiving Day, Christmas Day and New Years Day

- Adults: $17, Seniors & Veterans: $15, Kids 5 – 18: $8

www.Discover-Oregon.com

Fly in a Historic Biplane

There is a lot to discover in the Columbia River Gorge, but the highlight of any exploration would have to be taking to the skies and seeing the area's majestic beauty in a bright red 1942 Waco UPF-7 biplane!

Enjoy your up-front seat for two in the open cockpit as you fly around Hood River, soar above the Columbia River Gorge, and even take a flight around Mt. Hood during a longer excursion. It's an amazing Oregon adventure you'll never forget! Have a group of two or three? Then make the same flight in TacAero's enclosed Cessna 172 and ride all together.

Pricing per flight – (Not per person) – Up to 2 passengers:

    20 Minutes: $240 – Columbia River & Hood River
    45 Minutes: $450 – Hood River valley & Mt. Hood views

Note that reservations are required, and can be made by calling 844-359-2827. Please make your reservations at least one week in advance, and note that flights may be cancelled due to the weather. At least 24 hours advance notice is requested for any flight cancellations. The combined weight of two passengers cannot exceed 310 pounds.

    TacAero
    3608 Airport Road
    Hood River, OR 97031
    844-359-2827

- Open: Year-round – Monday through Saturday – Summer: 8:00 a.m. to 6:00 p.m. – Winter: 8:00 a.m. to 4:00 p.m.

Panorama Point

If you'd like to enjoy a panoramic view of Mt. Hood and the orchards and vineyards of the Hood River Valley, all without having to go for a hike, then Panorama Point is what you're after. Make the spiraling drive atop a small butte, park, and take in the views.

From the intersection of Historic Hwy 30 and Hwy 35 on the east side of Hood River, take Hwy 35 south for approximately 2 miles to Whiskey Creek Drive. Turn east here and follow this for ½ mile to Eastside Road. Turn north onto Eastside Road and follow this for ½ mile to the entrance for Panorama Point, on your left.

 Hood River Fruit Loop & Winery Tour

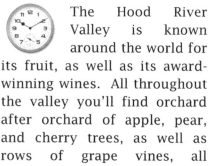 The Hood River Valley is known around the world for its fruit, as well as its award-winning wines. All throughout the valley you'll find orchard after orchard of apple, pear, and cherry trees, as well as rows of grape vines, all  growing their delicious fruit in the perfect Oregon summertime weather. Of course, you can't have fruit without pollination, and during the month of April, all of the orchards come to life in an explosion of pink and white blossoms, which is celebrated in a number of Hood River Blossom Festival events throughout the month. If you are visiting during April, check online beginning in March at http://hoodriver.org/celebrate-blossom-time-in-hood-river/ to see this year's schedule and dates.

And when summer comes to a close, then it's time for the fall harvest, and that calls for a celebration, as well. In addition to an abundance of fresh picked fruit and fine wines being offered all along the Fruit Loop, visitors will find the annual Hood River Valley Harvest Fest occurring for three days in mid-October down at the Event Site by the Columbia River. Visit www.HoodRiver.org/Harvest-Fest/ to learn about this year's dates, hours, and schedule of events.

Traversing all of these attractions is the **35-mile Fruit Loop**. This self-guided tour visits nearly 30 different farms, wineries and vineyards offering fresh fruit, jams, jellies, syrups, fruit smoothies, ciders, baked goods, flowers, local artisan gifts, and of course, award-winning wines. Pick up a Fruit Loop map while visiting local shops in Hood River, or download one online and plan on spending a couple of hours making the tour. *Mt. Hood and Barn Photo © Peter Marbach*

 Hood River Valley Lavender Farms

Colorful and aromatic, beautiful Lavender thrives in the Oregon climate. Visitors will often find acres of its blossoms neatly aligned in rows and beckoning artists, photographers, painters, and of course honey bees and bumble bees that are attracted to its pleasing scent and bright profusion of purple color. Lavender blooms for much of the summer in Oregon, and peaks during the month of July.

Here are two Lavender Farms located in Hood River Valley, both of which are on the Hood River Fruit Loop...

Hood River Lavender Farm – Fruit Loop Stop #10

With over 70 varieties of organic Lavender, the Hood River Lavender Farm offers acres of plants blooming in the shadow of Mt. Hood. In addition to being able to cut your own bouquets, visitors will find a large variety of Lavender related items for sale, including Lavender soap, tea, perfume, oils, culinary products, aromatherapy items, dried Lavender flowers and more.

Hood River Lavender Farms
3801 Straight Hill Road
Hood River, OR 97031
541-354-9917

- Open:

  May through September - Wednesday through Saturday – 10:00 a.m. to 5:00 p.m., Sunday 11:00 a.m. to 5:00 p.m.

  October – Friday and Saturday - 10:00 a.m. to 5:00 p.m., Sunday 11:00 a.m. to 5:00 p.m.

Lavender Valley – Fruit Loop Stop #17

Visit the Lavender Farm and cut a bouquet for yourself or loved ones, shop their farm stand for hand-crafted Lavender products made right there on the farm, or just bring a picnic lunch and enjoy the beautiful view of Mt. Hood.

Lavender Valley
5965 Boneboro Road
Mt. Hood Parkdale, OR 97041
541-386-1906

- Open: Late May through early September - Wednesday through Sunday – 10:00 a.m. to 5:00 p.m.

www.Discover-Oregon.com

The Hutson Museum

Located in a small building reflecting the historic 1900 Ries-Thompson home next door, the Hutson Museum offers an interesting mix of items showcasing the cultural and natural history of the area, including Native American artifacts, an impressive display of rocks and minerals, military items from WWI and WWII, and more. Admission: $1.00

The Hutson Museum
4967 Baseline Drive
Mt. Hood, OR 97041

- Open: 11:30 a.m. to 3:00 p.m. – Thursday through Sunday - April through October.

Driving Directions: While not listed on the tour map, the Hutson Museum can be found between Stops #14 and #15 on the Hood River Fruit Loop, on Baseline Drive.

Apple Valley Country Store

Huckleberries are kind of a big deal on Mt. Hood, and appearing as Stop #21 on The Fruit Loop is the Apple Valley Country Store & Bakery, which features hand-scooped huckleberry ice cream and milkshakes, as well as a wide selection of locally made items, including pies, jams, and jellies, all with fresh ingredients from local farmers. Inside, you'll find nice folks, and outside you'll find seating amongst the dahlias next to the Hood River. It's also a great place to stop at if you're cycling in the area.

Apple Valley Country Store
2363 Tucker Road
Hood River, OR 97031
541-386-1971

- Open: Wednesday through Saturday – 11:00 a.m. to 8:00 p.m.

Watch World Class Kiteboarders & Sailboarders

Hood River is one of the two best places in the world for kiteboarding and sailboarding, with the other being Hawaii. Visit the "Event Site" to park, get out and watch all of the action up close.

Driving Directions: From the corner of Oak Street and North 2nd Street in Hood River, proceed north on North 2nd Street as it crosses over I-84 and works its way down to the Event Site at the 0.4 mile mark.

Solstice Wood Fire Cafe & Bar

If it's time for lunch or dinner, then you'll want to check out one of our favorite places, Solstice Wood Fire Cafe & Bar. Down by the Event Center and always busy, it offers pizzas and Italian fare showcasing local and Pacific Northwest ingredients, all in a fun and friendly environment with heated outdoor seating, wood burning fireplaces, and river views.

Solstice Wood Fire Cafe & Bar
501 Portway Ave.
Hood River, OR 97301
541-436-0800

- Open: Sunday through Thursday – 11:00 a.m. to 8:30 p.m., Friday and Saturday – 11:00 a.m. to 9:00 p.m. Closed on Tuesdays during the winter.

History Museum of Hood River County

The Columbia River has been an important element in the history of this region for ages. With a course carved by ancient and powerful geologic and hydraulic forces, it has provided sustenance to Native Americans for countless generations, while its near sea-level path through the Cascade Mountain Range attracted early explorers, pioneers, farmers, trappers, and industrialists. Visit the History Museum of Hood River County to learn of the fascinating natural, cultural, agricultural, and recreational history of this region and the Columbia River Gorge.

The History Museum of Hood River County
300 E Port Marina Dr.
Hood River, OR 97031
541-386-6772

- Open: Monday through Saturday – 11:00 a.m. to 4:00 p.m. – Closed during the month of January.

MT. HOOD

You can't experience Hood River and much of the Columbia River Gorge without seeing majestic Mt. Hood towering to the south, beckoning visitors with its green forests, pristine rivers, and snowy alpine slopes.

The early days of exploration on Mt. Hood makes for a fascinating story, as rugged and determined individuals from all walks of life forged a difficult path to the mountain's northern and southern slopes, opening lodges, inns, restaurants, livery stables, transportation services and more to serve those who wished to make their way to the mountain, ski on its slopes, and in many cases climb to its 11,245' summit.

The following two destinations played an important role in Mt. Hood's early history and recreational development.

Cooper Spur Mountain Resort

Located at the base of Mt. Hood's northern slopes is the historic Cooper Spur Mountain Resort. This quaint resort offers travelers luxury lodge accommodations, mountain cabins, farm to table dining, and an abundance of year-round activities including downhill and Nordic skiing, all in a rustic mountain lodge setting.

Cooper Spur Mountain Resort
10755 Cooper Spur Road
Mt. Hood, OR 97041
541-352-6692

Historic Cloud Cap Inn

High on the eastern flank of Mt. Hood, at an elevation of 6,000', sits Cloud Cap Inn. Built in 1889 with hand-hewn timber and stone from the surrounding area, this historic mountain inn offers visitors dramatic up-close views of Mt. Hood, as well as Oregon's largest glacier, Eliot Glacier. With its centralized location, the inn is used as a base by the Crag Rats, a volunteer group providing rescues on Mt. Hood and the surrounding area, and as such, it is usually not open to the public, but visitors may get lucky when they stop by and find members of the Crag Rats stationed here and offering an opportunity to sit on the patio or peek inside. In addition, there are numerous trails leading from the inn to areas on the

east side of Mt. Hood, with the Cooper Spur hike being perhaps the most popular, as it takes hikers up and along the southern lateral moraine of the jumbled Eliot Glacier.

Early entrepreneurs opened the inn with the intention of it

becoming a luxury alpine resort. With its quality meals, feather bedding, and sublime mountain views, it commanded a premium price of $5 per night, thus attracting the well-to-do of society. However, reaching the inn proved to be quite
difficult, as the rough dirt road cut through the dense forest required four to five hours worth of arduous travel by horse-drawn stages to traverse. As a result, the original owners found few willing to make the journey. In the ensuing years, the building changed ownership a number of times, but began to slowly succumb to neglect in the harsh mountain environment. Violent winter storms, heavy spring snows, summer forest fires, and other battles with the elements began to take their toll on this unique building and it was eventually sold to the Forest Service in 1942. With World War II gripping the nation and all resources going to the war effort, the Forest Service had no time nor budget to maintain the inn, so they considered burning it down. However, in 1954 Oregon's Crag Rats, the oldest search and rescue team in the United States, purchased the inn for $2,000 and they have diligently maintained and cared for it ever since.

While the inn is generally not open to the public, official Forest Service guided tours for the public are offered at 11:00 a.m. and 1:00 p.m. on Sundays during the summer months until Labor Day weekend. For additional information and to sign up for a tour, call the
Hood River Ranger District at 541-352-6002. Their office is open Monday through Saturday during the summer, 8:00 a.m. to 4:30 p.m.

Driving Directions: From Hood River, proceed south on Hwy 35 for approximately 20 miles to Cooper Spur Road. Turn right / west onto Cooper Spur Road / Forest Service Road 3512 from Highway 35 and follow this for 2.3 miles to Cloud Cap Road. Turn left / south here and follow this for 11 miles as it turns into a dirt and gravel road making its way up through a burned forest filled with silver snags to a junction for the Tilly Jane Campground and the Cloud Cap Inn. Head right and follow this increasingly rough road for 1 mile as it curves up to the inn. Note that the road is very rough in places but is passable in a passenger car suited for this kind of travel. Visitors will need to display a Northwest Forest Pass on their car dashboard, and a free self-register wilderness permit will need to be filled out at the nearby trailheads if you'd like to do any hiking.

Important: Because of its elevation and unmaintained road, you will want to skip a visit to Cloud Cap Inn if you are traveling between October and mid- to late-June, or if there is *any* snow on the road to the inn. Note that there is no cell service on some sections of the road to Cloud Cap Inn.

For the latest road conditions, call:

- Hood River Ranger District – 541-352-6002
  - Open Monday – Saturday, 8:00 a.m. to 4:30 p.m.

Want to learn more about the history of Cloud Cap Inn, Timberline Lodge, Mt. Hood and the surrounding area? Then we highly recommend two web sites, www.MtHoodHistory.com and www.HistoricHoodRiver.com. Both are filled with rare and unique historical photos, ephemera, stories and personal accounts of days past that you cannot find anywhere else. Also, you'll want to check out the book *Mount Hood – Adventures of the Wy'east Climbers 1930 – 1942* by Ric Conrad.

Mosier Tunnels – Historic Columbia River Highway

MOSIER,
THE DALLES & DUFUR

MOSIER

Situated on the Historic Columbia River Highway / Historic Route 30, the small town of Mosier is host to one of the most interesting hikes in the entire Columbia River Gorge, the Mosier Twin Tunnels, as well as one of the best cycling routes in all of Oregon, the Mosier Twin Tunnels ride from Hood River to Rowena Crest / The Dalles and back. (I-84 - Exit 69)

 ## Mosier Twin Tunnels Hike – West Trailhead

 Closed to motorized traffic, the paved Historic Columbia River Highway State Trail takes visitors along the old Columbia River Highway to the Mosier Twin Tunnels, two impressive tunnels blasted into the basalt cliffside nearly 100 years ago. Inspired by the design of the Axenstrasse on Lake Lucerne, Switzerland, the tunnels were built with large viewing portals and observation walkways offering travelers a unique view of the gorge. Of note is the inscription carved into the rock on the north side wall at the east end of the tunnels. It reads...

Snowbound
November 19 to 27, 1921
Chas J. Sadilek
E. B Marvin

Note that an abundance of colorful wildflowers blooms in this area during the months of April and May, with the peak occurring in mid- to late-April. 8.5 Miles round trip.

Mosier Twin Tunnels Hike – East Trailhead

If you'd like a considerably shorter, yet still very scenic hike to the Mosier Twin Tunnels, begin from the trailhead located on the hike's eastern end. You'll hike the old Columbia River Highway among dramatic fields of basalt dotted with Ponderosa Pines and small oak trees while looking down on the Columbia River below. Approximately 2 miles round trip, depending on how much you choose to explore the tunnels.

Directions: West Trailhead

From I-84, take Exit 64 for Highway 35 to *White Salmon and Govt. Camp.* At the base of the exit, turn south and then follow the curved roadway 0.4 miles up to a 4-way stop. Turn left and wind your way up the hill for 1.2 miles to where the road ends at the trailhead parking area. A $5.00 parking fee is required here.

Directions: East Trailhead

Take I-84 to the Mosier Exit #69 and drive south from the off ramp. As the road drops and curves east toward Mosier, turn left onto Rock Creek Road and follow this back west up to the entrance road for the Historic Columbia Highway State Trail, which leads to the Mosier Tunnels. Do not turn here, but instead continue up and to your left, where you'll find parking. A $5.00 parking fee is required here.

Mosier Tunnels Ride

The eastern end of the Columbia River Gorge offers some of the finest cycling in all of Oregon, and the Mosier Tunnels route is one of the best rides in the state. Start with the unique Mosier Tunnels, throw in some amazing scenery, add the fact that you ride along the Historic Columbia River Highway for much of it, top it off with little to no automobile traffic, and you have a winner!

Most cyclists begin the ride at the Mosier Tunnels / Mark O. Hatfield West Trailhead, which is approximately 2 miles east of "Old Town" Hood River, on Old Columbia River Drive. (See the previous page.) Park at the trailhead, pay the $5 parking fee at the automated kiosk by the restrooms, and ride east along the paved path that is closed to cars, but open to pedestrians. Reach the Mosier Tunnels at 4 miles and enjoy the view from the viewpoint just beyond the east end of the tunnels before continuing on to the town of Mosier below, where you'll be joined by automobiles on the Historic Columbia River Highway as it casually winds its way past orchards, wineries, and scrub oaks out to Rowena Crest at just under 12 miles. This is a good turning around point, but if you want some additional mileage, drop down the Rowena Loops below Rowena Crest and continue on to The Dalles / The Columbia Gorge Discovery Center. (Note: Watch your speed on your descent of the Rowena Loops, as one of the rightward curves about ¾ the way down has a radius that tightens halfway through. Throw in a little too much speed, a bit of gravel on the pavement, and a stout guardrail, and things could get out of hand awfully quickly.) You'll want to be mindful of the wind forecast for this ride, as it can *sometimes* be a punishing headwind on the way back to the trailhead, especially during the summer months.

A nice option on your return (and if the wind kicks up a bit) is to turn left / south onto Marsh Cutoff Road (about halfway back) and follow this to State Road. Turn right here and enjoy a long descent into Mosier, ending up at the corner with Route 30 Classics & Roadside Refreshments...and their ice cream...on your left. (Funny how that worked out!) Note that you'll find a nice bike maintenance stand, complete with tools and a tire pump, at the west end of the small bridge in town.

 ## Mosier Plateau Trail

 A relatively short hike along Mosier Creek to the Mosier Plateau rewards hikers with both a waterfall and a grand view, and if you're here in April and May, you'll find colorful wildflowers, as well. Find the trail heading south at the east end of the old bridge in Mosier. Hike past Mosier Creek Falls, up four sets of stairs and switchbacks, and you're there. 3.5 Miles roundtrip, and approximately 2 miles if you hike to only the first viewpoint. Rated Moderate.

The trailhead for the Mosier Plateau Trail can be found on the right, immediately after passing the short narrow bridge when driving east through Mosier. Parking for a few cars can be found on the other side of the road, but if there are no spots available here, then return back west across the bridge and park in one of the large gravel lots with a sign for the Mosier Plateau Trail.

Mosier Valley Library

While you're in Mosier, be sure to stop in at what is perhaps the smallest library in the gorge, the historical 1913 Mosier Valley Library. Inside, you'll find an impressive collection of books, works by local authors, and historical photos from the area.

Mosier Valley Library
1003 3rd Avenue
Mosier, OR 97040

- Open: Tuesday through Friday - 2:00 p.m. to 4:00 p.m., Saturday - 10:00 a.m. to 12:00 p.m.

 ## Mosier Valley Post Office

 Located next door to the Mosier Valley Library, and housed in the 1914 Mosier Bank Building, is the quaint Mosier Post Office. Step inside to get a sense of the small building's history, and while there ask to see an interesting September, 1914 photo of Lenora Hunter, who served as Postmistress from 1910 to 1948.

Mosier Post Office
1001 3rd Ave.
Mosier, OR 97040

Mosier Farmers Market

If you're in Mosier on a Sunday anytime from 10:00 a.m. to 2:00 p.m. during the months of June through October, then be sure to stop in at the Mosier Farmers Market. Here, you'll find fresh produce, music, and handcrafted items by local artisans.

Mosier Saturday Market
Near 1202 1st Avenue
Mosier, OR 97040

 ## Mosier Waterfront Park – Rock Creek Trail

A pleasant stroll takes you on a wide trail with an unobstructed view of the Columbia River from Rock Creek Beach ½ mile east to Mosier Creek. Here, the trail passes back underneath I-84 before making its way west again along a narrow informal  trail on the south shore of small East Lake. Sit for a while on Rock Creek Beach or find a spot along the trail to watch sailboarders out on the water. About 1 mile roundtrip. Parking is available from May through October. ($5.00)

Driving Directions: Take Exit 69 and drive south. Immediately after the road curves east, turn left onto Rock Creek Road and follow this a short distance back west to the entrance for the Mosier Waterfront Park parking area on the right.

Route 30 Classics & Roadside Refreshments

After exploring the Mosier area, you're definitely going to want some hand-scooped ice cream, so head over to Route 30 Classics & Roadside Refreshments, decide on a single or double scoop with a waffle or sugar cone, and have a seat outside as you watch folks drive and cycle by.

Route 30 Classics & Roadside Refreshments
1100 1st Ave.
Mosier, OR 97040

- Open: Monday, Wednesday, Thursday & Sunday – 12:00 p.m. to 6:00 p.m., Friday & Saturday – 12:00 p.m. to 8:00 p.m., Closed Tuesdays.

 ## Memaloose Overlook

Stand at the Memaloose Overlook and gaze below to the northwest. There, in the center of the Columbia River, is Lower Memaloose Island, and standing at its edge is a 13' tall granite obelisk. This is the grave stone for Victor Trevitt. Born in 1827, he moved to The Dalles in 1853 and as a printer, entrepreneur, businessman, state legislator and the first judge to preside at the small Wasco County Courthouse, he played an important role in developing the town. Considering himself a friend of the Native Americans in the region, Mt. Trevitt requested that upon his death he be buried among their dead on Memaloose Island, an ancient burial ground holding burial vaults for the Native Americans who lived along the Columbia River. He died in 1883, at the age of 56, and was buried on the island in the spring of the following year.

You'll find the Memaloose Overlook on the Historic Columbia River Highway / Historic Route 30 approximately 2.7 miles east of Mosier, OR.

Rowena Crest Viewpoint / Tom McCall Nature Preserve

This "must stop" location gives travelers a commanding view of the east end of the Columbia River Gorge, a walk among spring wildflowers, and a high vantage point over the picturesque Rowena Loops of the old Columbia River Highway.

Note: Two short hikes may be made both above and below the parking area for Rowena Crest. The upper hike begins on the south side of the parking area and continues 1.8 miles to the summit of McCall Point. The lower trail, which begins to the west and opposite the turn into Rowena Crest, passes through wildflower meadows that bloom from late February through June, peaking in April and May. Early to mid-May offers an abundance of the brilliant yellow flowers of the Arrowleaf Balsamroot. Note that picking flowers is not permitted, and be mindful of the poison oak in this area, as well as ticks. In addition, dogs and bicycles are not allowed on these trails.

The Rowena Crest Viewpoint is located a little over 6 miles east of Mosier, OR on the Historic Columbia River Highway Scenic Byway / Hwy 30. To reach Mosier, take Exit 69 on I-84.

THE DALLES

During the mid-1800s, The Dalles was a major stop for pioneers on the Oregon Trail before they continued on a treacherous journey down the Columbia River to the Willamette Valley. Today, it offers travelers an abundance of outdoor adventure, including hiking, road cycling, gravel riding, sailboarding, fishing, and more, all as it showcases the ancient and dramatic history of the eastern end of the Columbia River Gorge, as reflected in its archaeological sites, historical buildings, old schoolhouses, ornate Victorian and Gothic style homes, and fine museums. (Exits 82, 83, 84, 85 & 87)

 Columbia Gorge Discovery Center & Museum

At over 48,000 square feet, the Columbia Gorge Discovery Center & Wasco County Historical Museum showcases a vast array of exhibits which explain the many wonders of this area, including the forces that shaped the Columbia River Gorge, the 10,000 year old culture of the gorge's native inhabitants, the journey of Lewis & Clark, and much more.

Columbia Gorge Discovery Center & Museum
5000 Discovery Drive
The Dalles, OR 97058
541-296-8600

- Admission: $9.00 – Ages 6 – 16: $5.00
- Open Daily: 9:00 a.m. – 5:00 p.m.

Raptor Interpretive Program – Columbia Gorge Discovery Center & Museum

The Columbia Gorge Discovery Center & Museum offers visitors a rare opportunity to see birds of prey, including eagles, owls, falcons and hawks, up close through its captivating Raptor Interpretive Program. Museum personnel present these majestic birds while explaining the challenges they face living in their gorge habitat. The program is free with the price of admission to the museum. *Photo © Oregon Department of Fish & Wildlife*

- Summer Hours: Daily - Mid-March to Mid-October 11:00 a.m. and 2:00 p.m.

- Fall and Winter Hours: 11:00 a.m. and 2:00 p.m. – Saturdays and Sundays only

Note that hours can vary slightly so as to accommodate group tours, so it is best if you call beforehand to confirm the day's schedule. 541-296-8600 – Ext 201.

 ## The Dalles Riverfront Trail

Traversing the south bank of the Columbia River for 10 paved miles between The Discovery Center on its west end and (eventually) The Dalles Dam Visitor Center on its east end, The Dalles Riverfront Trail makes for a nice stroll or bike ride along the Columbia River to downtown, Riverfront Park, The Dalles

Marina, and elsewhere. You'll find the western start of The Dalles Riverfront Trail at the entrance to the parking lot for the Columbia Gorge Discovery Center & Museum.

 ## Klindt's Booksellers

 The next chapter of your Columbia River Gorge exploration brings you to Klindt's Booksellers, the oldest bookstore in Oregon. Selling books since 1870, and from this bookstore since 1893, its shelves offer an abundance of titles, including an impressive collection of new books every month. You can even find our Oregon Road Trip and regional guidebooks here!

Klindt's Booksellers
315 E. 2nd Street
The Dalles, OR 97058
541-296-3355

- Open Monday – Saturday: 8:00 a.m. – 6:00 p.m.
- Sunday: 11:00 a.m. – 4:00 p.m.

 ## City of The Dalles Fire Museum

This small self-guided museum offers a unique taste of Oregon history with its two old-fashioned steam-powered fire engines from the 1800s, as well as an interesting collection of antique fire-fighting equipment, artifacts and photos.

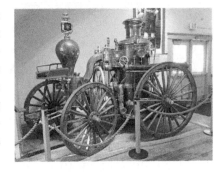

City of The Dalles Fire Museum
313 Court Street
The Dalles, OR 97058
541-296-5481 - xt 1119

- Located inside City Hall
- Free Admission
- Closed on Weekends
- Open Monday – Friday 8:00 a.m. – 5:00 p.m.

 National Neon Sign Museum

Located in the stately 1910 Elks Lodge in The Dalles is the National Neon Sign Museum. Here, you'll find a growing collection of colorful signs from the past, many of which you may recognize, and all arranged with interpretive displays that walk visitors  through the chronological history of store front advertising, beginning with the simple reflective signs of the mid-19th century before progressing to signs lit by the new incandescent light bulb in the late 1800s, with colorful neon then following in 1910. Be sure to make your way upstairs to walk among a collection of creative storefront facades, including Verne's Television Repair, Peggy's Beauty Shop, Chapman's Ice Cream, and, of course, Frank Neon Sign Co., all attracting customers with their colorful neon signs.

National Neon Sign Museum
200 East 3rd Street
The Dalles, OR 97058

- Open: Thursday through Saturday – 10:00 a.m. to 5:00 p.m.

 ## Old St. Peter's Landmark

The Old St. Peter's Landmark is a former Catholic Church that today serves as a beautiful historical museum. Built in 1897 with an ornate Gothic Revival architectural style, it features tall and colorful stained glass windows, a wooden Madonna carved from the keel of a sailing ship, imported Italian marble, and a towering spire which is the highest found in the Columbia River Gorge.

405 Lincoln Street
The Dalles, OR 97058
541-296-5686

- Free admission, Tuesday – Friday: 11:00 a.m. – 3:00 p.m., Saturday and Sunday: 1:00 p.m. – 3:00 p.m.

 ## Original Wasco County Courthouse

 Back in the mid-1800s, there was only one courthouse between the Cascades and the Rockies, and the Wasco County Courthouse was it! Built in 1859, the courthouse served as the Sheriff's Office, Clerk's Office, local church, courthouse and jail for a territory spanning over 130,000 square miles. Since then, it's served additional purposes while being moved six different times throughout The Dalles. Stop in at its current location to learn more about the important role this small courthouse has played in the history of the Pacific Northwest.

Original Wasco County Courthouse
410 West 2nd Place
The Dalles, OR 97058
541-296-4798

- Open May through September
- Thursday – Friday – Saturday – 11:00 a.m. to 3:00 p.m.

Fort Dalles Museum and Anderson Homestead

Dating back to 1905, the impressive Fort Dalles Museum is one of Oregon's two oldest history museums. Here you'll wander through a collection of original buildings from the 1856 Fort Dalles military compound, each offering a themed display of rare artifacts and items reflecting the amazing history of the area and its early pioneers. In addition, you'll find a barn filled with over 30 antique horse-drawn wagons and automobiles. Note: Be sure to ask to hear the working Edison Phonograph!

500 West 15th and Garrison
The Dalles, OR 97058
541-296-4547

- Admission: $8 – Students Ages 7 – 17: $1.00
- Open Monday – Sunday: 10:00 a.m. – 5:00 p.m. – March through November.
- Closed December, January and February.

 **Pulpit Rock**

If you want quirky, then you've found it with Pulpit Rock!

In the days of old, Pulpit Rock was one of a collection of small rocky "monoliths" scattered on an open hillside above The Dalles, with this one 12' tall rock being used by Methodist missionaries to deliver sermons during the 1840s. Today, it is surrounded by a residential neighborhood and acres of pavement. You'll find it located right in the middle of the intersection of Court Street and East 12th Street.

 Rorick House Museum

At over 165 years old, the small Malcolm A. Moody House, home of the Rorick House Museum, is the oldest remaining house in The Dalles.

The Rorick House Museum
300 W 13th St.
The Dalles, OR 97058
541-296-1867

- Open only during the summer months

 ## Sorosis Park

As you make your way about The Dalles, you can see high atop the hillside immediately to the south of town. You're probably thinking, "Wow, the view must be great from up there." You're absolutely right, it is! This hilltop is home to beautiful Sorosis Park, a 45 acre public park offering picnic tables, shade trees, a playground, tennis courts, softball fields, and of course, a stunning view of all of The Dalles, Mt. Adams, and the mighty Columbia River below.

 ## Nichols Art Glass

Stop in at Nichols Art Glass, grab a seat, and watch as Andy Nichols and his team practice their craft. As personable as he is skilled at the art of glassblowing, Andy will answer any questions you may have as he works to create pieces that are displayed in galleries, private collections, and exhibits around the world. His specialty is the creation of stunning salmon and trout, each of which takes 1.5 to 2 hours to bring to life.

Want a fun new holiday tradition? Then visit Nichols Art Glass to create your own Christmas ornament. Beginning the Friday after Thanksgiving, Andy and his staff help customers design and blow their very own unique glass ornament in a very hands on experience. It's great fun for the whole family. Early reservations are strongly recommended, and each ornament takes 30 to 40 minutes to complete.

Visitors to Nichols Art Glass are more than welcome, but call first to see if the shop is open and Andy or his staff will be blowing glass when you're in town. In a nutshell, Nichols Art Glass is open when it's open, so there are no set hours.

Nichols Art Glass
912 W 6th Street
The Dalles, OR 97058
541-296-2143

 ## Mama Jane's Pancake House

Located across the parking lot from Nichol's Art Glass, Mama Jane's Pancake House is always busy whenever we stop in for breakfast or lunch. The food is excellent, the portions are large, and the staff is friendly...and busy! Best of all, it's served up with a bit of an eclectic 1950s flavor.

Mama Jane's Pancake House
900 W 6th Street
The Dalles, OR 97058
541-296-6622

- Open: Daily – 6:00 a.m. to 2:00 p.m.

Sunshine Mill Artisan Plaza & Winery

Located near the east end of
The Dalles is the towering mill
building and silos of the
Sunshine Mill. Built more than
130 years ago to hold and mill
wheat harvested in eastern
Oregon, today it is home to
two wineries, Quenett and
Copa Di Vino, the leading

producer of premium wine by the glass in the United States.
Stop in to savor an impressive collection of vintages, enjoy
lunch at The Boiler House Bar, try your hand at a game of Bocce
Ball, or enjoy a warm summer evening while watching an
outdoor movie with your favorite new wine in hand.

Sunshine Mill Artisan Plaza & Winery
901 East Second Street
The Dalles, OR 97058
541-298-8900

- Open: 12:00 p.m. to 6:00 p.m. daily year-round.

 ## The Dalles Dam Visitor Center

The massive Dalles Dam is a
"powerhouse" for the region's
economy. Finished in 1957, it
has generated nearly 10 billion
kilowatt hours of electricity,
while facilitating the passage
of 10 million tons of river
cargo into and out of the
Pacific Northwest's Inland

Empire. Stop in at The Dalles Dam Visitor Center to view
interpretive displays which explain the impact of the dam from

numerous perspectives, including those of the world of agriculture, power, recreation, travel, fishing, and more. Then step outside to explore the over one mile of walking trails leading to the foundations of the old Seufert Cannery and its fish wheel, as well as the historic Seufert Rose Garden, which is home to more than 90 varieties of antique roses planted by Mrs. Seufert over 100 years ago. There is no admission charge for visiting the Visitor Center.

Free Tours of the Dam

 Free tours of the dam are also offered during the summer months, and these occur at 10:00 a.m. and 2:00 p.m. beginning in early May, though times can vary depending upon the availability of personnel. *Call the Visitor Center at least one day in advance to pre-register for the tours, as space is limited.*

The Dalles Dam Visitor Center
3545 Bret Clodfelter Way
The Dalles, OR 97058
541-296-9778

- Open: 9:00 a.m. to 5:00 p.m. - Weekends from May 1 through Memorial Day, and then every day through Labor Day. Open Friday through Sundays from Labor Day until the end of September.

The Eagles of Westrick Park

 Located north of The Dalles Dam Visitor Center, across the waterway, is Westrick Park, and every year bald eagles return here between mid- to late December and mid-February to roost in the trees and feed on shad in the river below. Ten years ago, one might have hoped to see 10 eagles roosting in these trees, but today you can spot as many as 60 during the peak period in mid-January!

To see the eagles, walk north of The Dalles Dam Visitor Center, across the parking lot, to the water's edge and look in the trees across the water, in front of the large concrete wall of the dam. Note: The Dalles Dam Visitor Center hosts an annual "Eagle Watch" event during the 3rd Saturday in January, when the eagles are most plentiful. If you didn't bring your own binoculars, you will find free stationary binoculars for viewing the eagles mounted atop posts in front of the Visitor Center. *Photo courtesy of Amber Tilton – US Army Corps of Engineers.*

 ## Big Jim's Drive-In

One place we really enjoy eating at in The Dalles, especially after a day of cycling in the area, is Big Jim's Drive-In. It's a family style restaurant offering sandwiches, soups, salads, hot dogs, and an amazing selection of hamburger choices, all made with fresh ingredients. You'll also find 16 flavors of Oregon's Umpqua ice cream, as  well as milk shakes, sundaes, fresh fruit smoothies and more.

Big Jim's Drive-In
2938 E. 2nd Street
The Dalles, OR 97058

- Open: Daily 10:00 a.m. to 10:00 p.m. – Open to 9:00 p.m. in the winter.

 ## Historic Petersburg Schoolhouse

A well-preserved historic one room school house that served students in The Dalles area. Note that it is not open to the public.

Historic Petersburg School
15 Mile Road
The Dalles, OR 97014

Driving Directions: From Big Jim's Drive-In in The Dalles, drive east on SE Frontage Road / State Road, which is next to Big Jim's, and follow this as it turns into Fifteen Mile Road. At 3.2 miles from Big Jim's, turn left / northeast onto what is still Fifteen Mile Road. (It's going to seem like Fifteen Mile Road continues straight, but that's now 8 Mile Road.) Drive 0.3 miles and find the school on the left.

 Note: The Historic Petersburg School House is a popular starting point for many outstanding cycling routes in this area, all of which head south and east from the school. For an excellent book of cycling routes in Oregon, we recommend *75 Classic Rides Oregon: The Best Road Biking Routes* by Jim Moore.

www.Discover-Oregon.com

A Whimsical Detour

Want to see a rafter (flock) of wild turkeys? Perhaps anywhere from 20 to 100 of them? Then leave the Petersburg School and return west on 15 Mile Road for 0.3 miles. Turn left / south onto 8 Mile road and immediately begin looking for wild turkeys in the field to your right, usually close to the tree line. If you don't see them here, continue driving a little further south on 8 Mile road, all the while looking for turkeys. You are most likely to see them within the first two miles after your turn. If you are unsuccessful, you may continue driving south on 8 Mile road, where you may spot a different rafter of wild turkeys on either side of the road anytime prior to reaching the five mile mark.

 ## Pathfinders Memorial

High on a road bank, clearly out of place among the wheat fields of the area, stands like a sentinel a single column of basalt. Affixed to its side is a bronze plaque, which reads... *Here lie many pathfinders to the Oregon country - Erected by The Wasco County Pioneer Association 1935.* This memorial is dedicated to those Oregon Trail pioneers who lost their lives and were buried in a burial ground adjacent to a nearby campsite used by early pioneers on their way to Fort Dalles in The Dalles.

Driving Directions: From the Historic Petersburg School House, continue east on Fifteen Mile Road for 6.7 miles. You'll spot the lone basalt column up on the bank to the left, just to the side of the road.

Deschutes River Trail Ride

 The eastern end of the Columbia River Gorge offers a wealth of cycling opportunities on both sides of the Columbia River, be they road, gravel or single-track, and the ride along the Deschutes River beginning at its confluence with the Columbia River is a casual classic almost anytime of the year!

On the east side of the mouth of the Deschutes River, where it flows into the Columbia River, is the Deschutes River State Park. Starting here and heading upriver is a 17 mile gravel route that follows a dirt road on the east bank of the Deschutes. Traversing an old rail bed, the road/trail is mostly level and double track, as well as closed to any motorized vehicles, making it perfect for cyclists, hikers, equestrians, fishermen, and others. All along its route you'll be accompanied by the cool flowing waters of the Deschutes River, which cuts its course through dramatic cliffs and towering hillsides, open fields crossed by barbed-wire fences, and tree-lined banks offering shade, all providing captivating scenery along the way. Listen for the Western Meadowlark or Red-Winged Blackbird as you ride, enjoy the early season wildflowers, perhaps spot an owl late in the day, and keep an eye out for snakes, including gopher snakes sunning

themselves on the trail (don't run over that "stick") and rattle snakes tucked amongst the rocks. It's highly unlikely you'll spot a rattlesnake while riding, but if you hike toward the river, you *may* find one in the rocks. If you hear a rattle, head the other way.

Riding your bike is an excellent way to experience this long scenic stretch of the Deschutes River with a degree of solitude, save for the occasional train rumbling by on the opposite shore. It's also a great overnight adventure. Just put a pack on your back, hop on your bike and ride.

Note: An Oregon State Parks parking permit is required to park at the trailhead here. You'll also want to check the wind forecast, as a stout afternoon headwind will oftentimes blow on your return ride, and *be sure to carry a functional patch kit with you*, as the sharp spines of goat head seeds will puncture your tires if you journey *off trail* further up the river. There is no potable water along this route, so be sure to bring plenty of liquids with you, especially during the hot summer months.

Maryhill Museum of Art

MARYHILL, SCHREINER FARMS, LYLE & BINGEN

MARYHILL

"The Land Where the Rain and Sunshine Meet"

Many of the attractions you see in the Columbia River Gorge have a history tied to Sam Hill, the builder of the Columbia River Highway, America's first Scenic Highway, which was dedicated in June of 1916. Serving as President of the Washington State Good Roads Association, he was an active and influential proponent for the construction of good roads throughout Oregon, the northwest, and elsewhere. As part of his dreams and endeavors, he built the Maryhill Loops Road, an experimental road which he used to influence the Oregon Governor, Oswald West, and the State Legislature to allocate the funds and resources necessary for the construction of the Columbia River Highway.

After the construction of his Maryhill Loops Road, Sam Hill set out to build his home, which being grand in design, was to be the centerpiece of his Maryhill community, home to a store, post office, church, blacksmith's shop, an Inn, and acres of fruit trees. Built of thick cement, he stated *"I expect this house to be here for a thousand years after I am gone."* Unfortunately, the lack of available water in this arid climate caused his dreams of building a town to fail, and in 1917 he ceased construction on his home. In 1920, a friend of his, Loie Fuller, convinced him to finish his home and convert it into a world-class museum. Today, it is known as the Maryhill Museum, and its impressive collection includes works from around the world and features more than 80 pieces by French sculptor Auguste Rodin.

Stonehenge WWI Memorial

Standing east of Maryhill, Washington is a replica of England's famous Stonehenge. Built by Sam Hill and completed in 1929, thirteen years after he finished the Columbia River Highway, it serves as a memorial to the 13 young men from Klickitat County who gave their lives for our country and our freedom during World War I. Nearby, you will also find a memorial dedicated to those soldiers from Klickitat County who have given their lives since that time.

Note that you'll find the tomb of Sam Hill 50 yards to the south of the Stonehenge WWI Memorial, just below a rim of basalt and overlooking the Columbia River.

To reach the Stonehenge WWI Memorial, travel on I-84 to Exit 104. Exit here and turn north to cross over the Columbia River. Soon after crossing the bridge, turn right / east toward the Maryhill State Park – Heritage Site and stay on this road for 1.1 miles until you turn left / north onto Stonehenge Drive. Follow Stonehenge Drive for 0.9 miles to the entrance to the memorial.

Maryhill Loops Road Overlook

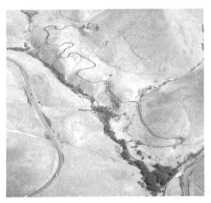

Prior to the construction of the Columbia River Highway, the highway's builder, Sam Hill, and chief architect, Samuel Lancaster, built in 1911 an experimental road that snaked down a hillside toward the Columbia River, east of the Maryhill Museum. At the time, it was a masterpiece in design and execution, and its purpose was to convince the Governor of Oregon and members of the state legislature to support Sam Hill's vision for building the Columbia River Highway. Mr. Hill's idea worked, and soon he was building *"...a great highway so that the world can realize the magnificence and grandeur of the Columbia River Gorge."*

The Maryhill Loops Road is open to non-motorized use only, and this is between the hours of 7:00 a.m. to 5:00 p.m. There is no admission fee. Access the road from its southern end, off of Highway 14.

To reach the Maryhill Loops Road overlook, travel on I-84 to Exit 104. Exit here and turn north to cross over the Columbia River. Continue north on Hwy 97, (briefly taking a leftward "jog" on Hwy 14 at the 1.8 mile mark) until you reach the entrance for the overlook on your right at 4.6 miles after crossing the Columbia River.

To reach the south entrance to the Maryhill Loops, follow Hwy 97 north to Hwy 14 after crossing the Columbia River. Turn right onto Hwy 14 and follow this a little over 1 mile to the entrance on your left.

www.Discover-Oregon.com

Goldendale Mountain Identifier

Just north from the Maryhill Loops on Hwy 97 is the Goldendale Mountain Identifier. A large paved pullout on the west side of Hwy 97, it offers a panoramic view of the vast Klickitat Valley as well as a rare sighting of Mt. Hood, Mt. Adams, Mt. St. Helens, and Mt. Rainier all in the same view.

To reach the Goldendale Mountain Identifier, travel on I-84 to Exit 104. Exit here and turn north to cross over the Columbia River. Continue north on Hwy 97, (briefly taking a leftward "jog" on Hwy 14 at the 1.8 mile mark) until you reach the parking area for the Golden Mountain Identifier on your left at 7.2 miles after crossing the Columbia River.

 ## Lewis & Clark Overlook

An impressive observation point with interpretive signs overlooking the Columbia River immediately east of the Maryhill Museum parking area.

Lewis and Clark Overlook
57 Maryhill Museum Drive
Goldendale, WA 98620

- Open: Daily – 10:00 a.m. to 5:00 p.m.

Maryhill Museum of Art

Sitting on park-like grounds high above the Columbia River is the regal Maryhill Museum of Art. Built by Sam Hill and dedicated in 1926 by Queen Marie of Romania, it opened to the public in 1940 and today offers visitors an impressive collection of paintings, sculptures and furniture from around the world, including works by Auguste Rodin, as well as a beautiful display of Native American artifacts.

Admission:

- Adults: $12.00
- Seniors 65 and older: $10
- College: $9
- Youth 7 to 18: $5 (Children 6 and under are free)
- Family: $30 (2 Adults and related children 7 to 18)
- Show your receipt from any Columbia Gorge wine tasting room and receive a $2 discount off your admission.

Maryhill Museum of Art
35 Maryhill Museum Drive
Goldendale, WA 98620
509-773-3733

- Open: Daily – 10:00 a.m. to 5:00 p.m. - March 15 to November 15
- Loïe's Café – Inside the Museum – Open 10:30 a.m. to 4:30 p.m.

www.Discover-Oregon.com

Maryhill Winery

Opened in 2001, the award-winning Maryhill Winery offers its visitors a world-class collection of fine wines, all in an impressive setting high above the Columbia River. Take a seat on the patio and savor a selection of vintages while enjoying the sunshine  and taking in the view of 11,245' Mt. Hood in the distance. Be sure to head back this way in the future to enjoy warm evenings while listening to performers in its world-class summer concert series.

Enjoy yourself, but do remember that you are driving today, so be sure to taste wines in moderation.

Maryhill Winery
9774 Hwy 14
Goldendale, WA 98620
509-773-1976

- Open: Daily – 10:00 a.m. to 6:00 p.m.

 Horsethief Butte

As you travel along Highway 14, you'll come upon the massive Horsethief Butte to the south. A handful of trails from the parking area will take you around the perimeter of the butte to its south side, where you'll find amazing views of the Columbia River, or  up "into" the butte, where you can explore a maze of narrow "slots" or make your way atop the walls to enjoy the view. It's also likely that you'll find rock climbers here in the spring and fall, especially on the interior walls.

To reach Horsethief Butte, take Exit 87 from I-84 and cross The Dalles Bridge. Continue approximately 2.5 miles after crossing the bridge to Hwy 14. Turn right / east onto Hwy 14 and proceed 2.8 miles to the parking for Horsethief Butte. Note that a Discovery Pass is required for parking here, and a day pass or annual pass may be purchased at the parking lot kiosk. Remember to keep an eye out for poison oak.

 ## Spearfish Park and Spearfish Lake

Popular with the locals, Spearfish Lake is a great fishing spot for kids and adults alike. Every year, sometime in late December to early January, the lake is planted with several thousand rainbow trout, plus over one hundred broodstock rainbows reaching to 11 lbs.! Note that a Washington fishing license is required to fish here.

In addition, hikers will find a 2.2 mile four-season loop trail that makes its way around the lake. Elevation gain: 45'

You'll find Spearfish Park immediately north of The Dalles Dam, on the Washington side of the Columbia River. From Hwy 197, turn east onto East Dock Road and follow this to its end to find access to Spearfish Park and Spearfish Lake.

 **Hess Park**

Follow a short trail to Hess Park where you'll find not only a pond, but also an active beaver den, along with a lot of gnawed upon trees! *Do not approach nor bother the den.*

To reach Hess Park, turn east onto a gravel road that leads south next to Hwy 197, north of The Dalles Dam and just south of East Dock Road, and follow this to a large parking area.

 Schreiner Farms

"Am I seeing what I think I'm seeing?!"

Take a right off of Hwy 14 onto Schreiner Farms Road and instantly find yourself in Asia, Australia or even Africa! You're now entering the 12,000 acre Schreiner Farms, an operating cattle ranch with over 400 cattle, as well as an amazing collection of exotic

animals, including Giraffes, Wallaroos, Zebras, Camels, Bison, Ostriches, Emus, Elk, Turkeys, Geese, Antelope and many others, all wandering about in wide open areas.

Being a private ranch, Schreiner Farms is not a zoo, and you cannot walk about. That said, you are more than welcome to turn up Schreiner Farms Road from Hwy 14 and travel its ½ mile length while spotting animals from your car. Heed the signs stating that you must remain in your vehicle and turn around once you've reached the Giraffe Barn. Note that the

animals are most active in the early and latter parts of the day during the warm spring and summer months, or throughout the day during the cooler fall and winter months.

Since you are a guest, please be respectful of the animals, the owners, the ranch hands and any other visitors. Drive slowly and quietly, and please do not honk your horn.

Schreiner Farms
Schreiner Farms Road
Lyle, WA 98635
509-448-4580

- Usually open during daylight hours

Note: As you approach and leave Schreiner Farms on Highway 14, keep an eye out for exotic animals roaming in the fields on the north side of the highway.

LYLE

 ## Klickitat Trail – Lyle Trailhead

Beginning near the confluence of the Klickitat and Columbia rivers, in the small town of Lyle, is the Klickitat Trail. Following a former rail bed for the Spokane, Portland & Seattle Railway, this rails to trail route winds its way for 31 miles up to the grassy open plains of the Goldendale Plateau, first passing through oaks and pines along the wild and scenic Klickitat River to the town of Klickitat, WA, before following Swale Creek up into the narrow Swale Canyon and then onto the plateau.

Painstakingly restored by the diligent efforts of the Klickitat Trail Conservancy, the trail makes for a nice hike. Park at the paved parking area and explore upriver before turning around. As an option, drive up two-lane Hwy 42 along the Klickitat

River for 1.6 miles to a small turn out on your left for a large wooden trestle. (Just before Fisher Hill Road) The view of the river from the restored pedestrian friendly trestle as it flows through a narrow channel far below is worth the short drive. (Photo)

Note that the gravel Klickitat Trail is also an excellent mountain bike ride. Consider riding up river from the trailhead in Lyle, or drive up to the opposite end of the trail, to the trailhead off of Harm's Road, just off the Centerville Highway on the Goldendale Plateau northeast of here, and make your way downriver through open meadows before descending the slight grade into Swale Canyon, (Photo) an area rich in wildflowers and song birds in the spring. Of course, be mindful of ticks, rattlesnakes and poison oak.

 For road cyclists, the ride from Lyle up Hwy 42 along the Klickitat River east to Goldendale, WA, and then back west along the Centerville Hwy makes for a challenging yet scenic 68 mile loop ride finishing with a fast descent back into Lyle. Be mindful of the wind forecast, as a strong headwind can blow during the latter half of the ride along the Centerville Hwy.

You'll find parking (with restrooms) for the Klickitat Trail at the west end of Lyle, just off of Hwy 14.

 Bald Eagles on the Balfour-Klickitat Loop Trail

You can spot a small number of "resident" bald eagles throughout the gorge year-round, but between mid- to late December through mid-February, their numbers increase significantly as they migrate here from nearby states in search of milder weather and a source of winter food, which includes a variety of fish from the Columbia River. A well-known feeding ground is the Klickitat Cove, just off the Klickitat River at Lyle. Here, *during the winter months*, you can spot adult and juvenile bald eagles perched in the trees around the cove as they watch the migrating salmon below. You can expect to see anywhere from a few eagles to as many as 60. We usually will see a handful in the trees, with perhaps a dozen soaring above. Keep an eye out for them up in the trees as you hike *to* the cove, and be sure to bring your binoculars when you visit.

To reach the cove, turn north off of Hwy 14 onto Old Hwy 8 (Just *west* of the bridge leading into Lyle) and follow this uphill for 0.2 miles to the small parking area for the **Balfour-Klickitat Loop Trail** on your right. Park here and take the paved trail on the left,  which will eventually turn to dirt, from the parking area to the cove. The .75 mile (roundtrip) trail is an easy hike. Note that the paved trail to the right ultimately connects with the trail leading left so as to create a loop. This nice short trail offers some views of the Klickitat River and impressive up close views of majestic old oaks.

Photo courtesy of Amber Tilton – US Army Corps of Engineers.

 Osage Orange Trees at Balfour

Adjacent to the east end of the parking area for the Balfour Klickitat Loop Trail (above) is an informal row of scraggly looking large trees leading north to south. At first glance, these appear to be simply some old trees, but they are actually a unique feature of the  gorge, for these are Osage Orange trees. Growing to a height reaching 50', these trees, with their deeply furrowed bark and yellow wood twice as dense as that of oak, are known for their unique fruit, the Osage Orange. Prior to the first use of barbed-wire in 1874, settlers to this area would plant these trees and keep them pruned so as to create a large hedge that was "horse-high, bull-strong, and pig-tight" for keeping free-range livestock and other animals corralled to certain areas. Native Americans highly prized the tree's strong, flexible, and durable wood for making bows and arrows, and they would travel great distances to obtain it. The "oranges" of the tree, which ripen in September and October, and last into January, are not actually oranges, but instead an inedible non-poisonous fruit from the mulberry family. Because of their dense nature, livestock will give them a pass, though small animals, such as squirrels, will eat their seeds.

To see the trees, turn north off of Hwy 14 onto Old Hwy 8 (Just *west* of the bridge leading into Lyle) and follow this uphill for 0.2 miles to the small parking area for the Balfour-Klickitat Loop Trail on your right. Park here, and you'll see the trees adjacent to the trailhead.

 Twin Bridges Museum

 Located just north of Hwy 14 in Lyle is the small Twin Bridges Museum. Step inside to explore the history of the Lyle area, its current and former inhabitants, the lives of Native Americans in the gorge and more, all through a collection of interesting displays featuring artifacts, photos, tools, and even an old wooden washing machine.

Twin Bridges Museum
403 Klickitat Street
Lyle, WA 98635

- Open: Every Saturday – 12:00 p.m. to 5:00 p.m. – June through Sept. Also by appointment: 509-365-3903.

Catherine Creek Trail & Spring Wildflowers

The skies cry "Winter!", while the earth whispers "Spring."

Every winter, explorers of the Columbia River Gorge wait for the appearance of the very first wildflowers. This is often the vibrant Grass Widow, which defiantly blooms in the cold winds and blowing snow to whisper that spring is on its way.

The wildflowers of Catherine Creek are some of the earliest to bloom at the eastern end of the Columbia River Gorge, with the first wildflowers of the year beginning to appear in January. Come April and May, you'll find entire hillsides covered in bright colorful flowers, including the dramatic yellow Arrowleaf Balsamroot. (Photo)

The northward leading **Catherine Creek Trail** climbs (hopefully sunny) south facing slopes offering beautiful views of the Gorge. 1.9 Miles round-trip with 325' of elevation gain.

Note that across Old Highway 8 you'll find a nice double set of paved loops meandering among open bluffs and old gnarled oaks to captivating views of the river and occasional benches upon which to sit and enjoy them. Caution: *Please be careful when crossing Old Highway 8!*

To reach the trailhead, travel Hwy 14 for 4.5 miles east of Bingen, WA and turn left / north onto Old Hwy 8, along the west shore of Rowland Lake. Proceed on Old Hwy 8 for 1.5 miles to the large gravel parking area for Catherine Creek.

BINGEN

Located on the northern shore of the Columbia River, opposite Hood River, the small town of Bingen, Washington is the launching point for an abundance of outdoor activities, including road cycling, mountain biking, kayaking, rafting, hiking, horseback riding, fishing, and of course, sailboarding and kiteboarding.

 Antiques & Oddities

An "antiques destination" in the gorge for more than 25 years, Antiques & Oddities is filled with an eclectic collection of quality antiques from around the area and the Northwest, as well as Asia and Europe. If you stop in, be sure to head downstairs.

Full disclosure...Antiques & Oddities is owned by our very good friend, Steve Wolford, whom we've known for many years. Tell Steve we sent you.

Antiques & Oddities
211 W. Steuben St.
Bingen, WA 98605
509-493-4242

- Open: Daily - Year-round – 10:00 a.m. to 5:00 p.m.

Gorge Heritage Museum

Dedicated to preserving the history of Bingen, White Salmon, and the surrounding area, the Gorge Heritage Museum welcomes visitors with an impressive collection of artifacts and exhibits reflecting the lives of Native Americans and early pioneers of the area. Here, visitors will find Native American artifacts, pioneer clothing and household items, ranching, farming and logging tools, interesting historical documents and photos, and a fascinating country store exhibit stocked with hundreds of old-fashioned products. Admission is $5.00.

Gorge Heritage Museum
202 E Humbolt St.
Bingen, WA 98605
509-493-3228

* Open: May through September – 12:00 p.m. to 5:00 p.m. – Friday, Saturday & Sunday. Winter Hours: Available by appointment. Contact via email at least 3 days prior to your arrival. ghm@gorge.net

The Glenwood Grade Cycling Route

Another classic road ride in the Columbia River Gorge is the 42-mile "Glenwood Grade." Offering a mix of hills, rollers, flat roads and countless scenic vistas of ever-changing Mt. Adams, the Glenwood Grade is a go-to ride for many cyclists in this part of the gorge.

Directions: Drive to BZ Corner (north of White Salmon, WA on Hwy 141 / Trout Lake Hwy) and park in the large parking area north of the single main intersection in BZ Corner. (The White Salmon River - BZ Corner Boating Site) Ride south a short distance from the parking area and turn left / east at the main intersection onto the BZ – Glenwood Highway. Follow this for 20 miles to Glenwood, WA, where you can refuel at the local bike-friendly restaurant or grocery store. From here, proceed west out of town on the Trout Lake Hwy past the Conboy Wildlife Refuge and over the "Triple Summit", (It's actually 6 hills, if you count them all) and then drop down to Sunnyside Road. (Mind the gravel on the road by the quarry on the long descent from the last summit.) Turn left / south onto Sunnyside Road and follow this back to Hwy 141 / Trout Lake Hwy, or skip turning onto Sunnyside Road and continue west to Trout Lake, WA before heading south on Hwy 141 / Trout Lake Hwy back to BZ Corner.

 ## Columbia River Viewpoint

One of the great things about the Columbia River Gorge is *seeing* the Columbia River Gorge. Here's an outstanding vantage point from high on the north side of the river, across from Hood River, where you can see far to the east as the river winds its way toward  you, across to the hidden cliffs and coves on the south shore, and out over the multitude of colorful kiteboarders and sailboarders catching the wind below. Oh, and instead of hiking to this spot, you drive to it. *Photo by Robert Kroese.*

To reach the viewpoint, turn north onto Cook-Underwood Road, which is 1.7 miles west of the north end of the Hood River Bridge across the Columbia, and follow this for 3 miles to a large gravel pullout on the south side of the road.

Dog Creek Falls

A short one minute hike brings you to Dog Creek Falls. Unlike the falls on the south side of the Columbia River, the 25' high cascade of Dog Creek Falls is often in the sunshine. Look for the falls to be flowing pretty good during the winter and spring months, while tapering off in the summer and fall. With such a nice reward for a short hike, this is a "must see" destination.

You'll find Dog Creek Falls 9.3 miles west of the north end of the Hood River Bridge across the Columbia. Look for a large gravel parking area on the right next to Hwy 14, just behind a guardrail. If you're traveling west and drive past the parking area, (it comes up quick) don't worry, as there is a pullout just up ahead where you can turn around.

The Oregon Pony – First steam locomotive used in the Oregon Territory

STEVENSON, BONNEVILLE & BEACON ROCK

STEVENSON, BONNEVILLE & BEACON ROCK

Stevenson Waterfront Path

The wide section of the Columbia River which flows past Stevenson on the north shore and Cascade Locks to the south is one of the most scenic areas of the entire gorge. Thunder Island in Cascade Locks is the perfect spot for an afternoon or evening picnic as you watch barges, sailboats, and other craft ply the water from a soft green lawn in the shade, while the paved Stevenson Waterfront Path on the north shore offers a nice stroll in the sunshine. Here, you can dip your toes in the water, sit on a bench while watching a sternwheeler arrive, and see expert kiteboarders and sailboarders shred the waves as they catch the wind.

Part of the Stevenson Interpretive Trails network, the 0.5 mile-long Stevenson Waterfront Path extends from west of the Stevenson Landing pier east to the Cascade Boat Launch. To access it, park at Bob's Beach, in the large street parking area near the Stevenson Landing, or at the Cascade Boat Launch.

Stevenson Farmers Market

Did you know the average vegetable travels more than 7 days and 1,500 miles before it lands on a grocer's shelf? Not with the Stevenson Farmers Market! Stop by on any Saturday between mid-June to mid-October and pick up regionally grown produce and fresh farm products sold by the actual farmers manning the booths. You'll also find many different items hand-crafted by local artisans, as well as some live music. Located by the river, adjacent to the Stevenson Waterfront Path.

- Saturdays – 10:00 a.m. to 2:00 p.m.
- Mid-June to Mid-October

Stevenson Waterfront Farmers Market
140 SW Cascade Avenue
Stevenson, WA 98648
509-427-4707

By the way, if you're hungry while visiting the Stevenson Farmers Market or Waterfront Path, stop in at **Clark & Lewie's** near the Stevenson Landing and enjoy a bite to eat for lunch or dinner while sitting on their outdoor patio admiring the river view.

Clark & Lewie's Travelers Rest Saloon & Grill
130 SW Cascade Ave.
Stevenson, WA 98648
509-219-0097

Benjamin & Mary Frazer (Frazier)

Benjamin Frazer
Born 1841
Died January 1, 1914

Mary Frazer
Born 1838
Died October 19, 1913

It's nearly impossible to explore the Columbia River Gorge without seeing the ever-present elements of gorge history. The captivating stories of the Historic Columbia River Highway seem to reveal themselves with every turn in the old road, while echoes from the steam whistles of railroads and steamships past remind us of the small towns and settlements that once thrived at the river's edge but are no more, and the numerous small museums dotting both sides of the river bring to life again the artifacts of the Native Americans and early pioneers who lived for generations in the area.

When looking at the history of the gorge, it's easy to see only the towns, buildings, steam trains, sternwheelers, and even fish wheels of the days gone by. Peering closer, however, you begin to get a sense of the lives of the people who came before us, those who lived in the gorge and built the towns, drove the trains, piloted the sternwheelers, ran the hotels, stocked the general stores, and even turned the muddy faint trails into roadways. More than just historical figures or faces in a photograph, their lives were rich and varied, filled with stories of hardship, perseverance, success, setbacks, love, and romance. It's interesting to consider that many of the people you see in the old photos found in gorge museums today are buried in the small cemeteries found alongside the river.

What follows is the tale of two gorge pioneers laid to rest at the Stevenson Cemetery, Benjamin and Mary Frazer, as told in an article titled *Stories the Tombstones Do Not Tell*, by Daphne Ramsay, and as published in Jim Atwell's 1974 book, *Columbia River Gorge History - Volume Two*...

Benjamin Frazer packed up his fiddle and a few possibles and headed west. He was a soldier in the Union Army; but he was young and impatient and he did not wait to be mustered out.

Benjamin loved to play his fiddle at dances and play-parties, and one night he met Mary, a girl who loved to dance.

Their romance was suddenly so intense that they planned to run away together. Mary had a husband and several small children. One can only speculate about Mary's reasons, but the story goes that Mary's husband had raised some hogs and planned to take them to market on a certain morning very early.

Mary told Benjamin she would leave a lamp burning in the window on the night she knew her husband would leave. The husband went his unsuspecting way, and Mary kissed each sleeping child and went to join Benjamin, who waited with two riding horses not far away.

They left, never to return: Mary never saw her children again.

It is unfortunate that my story has so few details of their long trip to our community, but I am recalling bits and pieces told me by people who knew them after they came to live in Skamania County.

They owned property now comprising the Interlaken and Bowles Lakes. Their home stood for many years in the vicinity of Ash's Lake.

I have been told that they changed their names to Bently and Mary Geer, and that with Elmer Ash, they operated a store in the settlement there that was called "Bagdad" in the vicinity of the present-day Co-Ply mill.

Bent Geer was a drinker and at times would confide the secrets of his past.

He would cry and lament that he could never go home again; he was a deserter from the army and had stolen another man's wife.

He always wore a gun because he feared he would be tracked down. Stevenson's main street below the railroad tracks was well supplied with saloons in those days and it was a common occurrence for Bent Geer's team and wagon to stand in front of one or another of them.

The barkeeper would assist Bent out of the saloon, load him in his wagon and untie the horses. The patient team knew the way home and always delivered him safely to Mary.

Her neighbors knew her as Molly. Agatha Garwood told me that she remembered seeing Molly sitting on her little porch smoking her pipe.

It seemed that Molly was deeply fond of Bent. Ethel Patterson recalls that Lizzie Fields, a neighbor of Molly in those long gone days, told her that they would pick blackberries to sell across the river at Cascade Locks. He would take them in his rowboat, and Molly would stand on the bank and call out to him, "Good-bye, Hon!" as he rowed away.

Hard times befell the Geers in their old age. They sold their property below Stevenson and went to live on the old John Anderson homestead (we know it as the Dodge place) on the loop road.

At the last they were county charges and Clarence Walker looked after them as they became feeble.

Do you think it was all worth it to Mary? Was her life with Bent Geer what she really wanted? I cannot help thinking that she may have shed many bitter tears.

Several years after their death, in the 1920s, a man came to Stevenson in search of his mother. I do not know how he traced her here, except that he had inquired at Fort Hall.

An Indian there remembered the man and woman who had passed without stopping-unusual enough to remember at this remote and lonely outpost! It was a long way to another stopping place.

It is also possible that Mary wrote to someone back home, but I do not know how her son traced her here to Stevenson.

Unfortunately, the people he spoke to did not know the story I have just told and he went away without ever knowing his mother was here.

It might have been a comfort to him to know that his mother was at rest in a peaceful, small cemetery with a respectable marker.

You'll find Benjamin and Mary's two small rectangular granite block gravestones in the Stevenson Cemetery, to the south of the road which loops through the grounds. Look for them to the right of the tall obelisk gravestone for Samuel L. Moore, near a low wall marking another grave's plot.

Skamania Lodge

With its large timbers, warm wood paneling, Mission-style furnishings, hand-crafted stonework, and black wrought iron accents, the 4-story Skamania Lodge is reminiscent of the historic grand lodges of America's National Parks. Visitors may relax with a book in front of the three-story stone fireplace, watch a warm summer evening fade into night from the great lawn while enjoying a sweeping view of the Columbia River, or take one of the three short hikes around the 18-hole par 70 golf course located amidst towering firs and a couple of large mountain ponds, each complete with basking turtles.

Skamania Lodge Zip Line

Take to the air on 7 different zip lines and 3 sky bridges as you make your way through a canopy of fir trees. You've never zip lined before? That's not a problem. Experienced guides will lead you through the entire course to make sure you have the time of your life!

- $99 Per person
- No age limit
- Requires approximately 2.5 hours to complete
- Zip lines take flight throughout the day – Call for times.
- Reservations are highly recommended – Call 509-427-0202 or visit www.ZipnSkamania.com - It is best to make reservations up to a week in advance, especially during summer weekends and holidays, though walk ups are sometimes available, so feel free to inquire.

Check in for your adventure at the Skamania Lodge Adventures office, which may be found in the conference center foyer of Skamania Lodge.

 ## Skamania Lodge Aerial Park

 This lofty challenge course tests your strength, coordination, and balance as you make your way through 19 platforms and 23 trials of varying degrees of difficulty...and courage! Don't worry, however, as you're clipped in with a redundancy system, so you can never fall. While there are Park Monitors, you may guide yourself through the course at your own pace.

- $69 Per person
- Minimum 6 years of age
- Ages 6 through 8 must have a guardian at a 1:1 ratio
- Children over 8 must be able to reach up to 6 feet high
- No open toed shoes allowed
- Maximum weight limit: 275 lbs.
- Requires approximately 2.0 hours
- Reservations are highly recommended - Call 509-427-0202 or visit www.ZipnSkamania.com

Skamania Lodge Adventures
1131 Skamania Lodge Way
Stevenson, WA 98648
509-427-0202

Check in for your adventure at the Skamania Lodge Adventures office, which may be found in the conference center foyer of Skamania Lodge.

Columbia Gorge Interpretive Center

The Columbia River Gorge has been shaped by both powerful geological events and fascinating cultural history for thousands of years. Visit the Columbia Gorge Interpretive Center to get an understanding of these events, the history of the gorge's first inhabitants, the Cascade Chinook Native Americans, and the more recent history dating back to the 1800s. Impressively-curated displays convey the story behind the lives of early fur trappers, explorers, and settlers, as well as the early logging industry, the role of fishing for salmon and sturgeon, the influence of the SP&S Railway that made its way through the gorge, the journey of Lewis & Clark, and more.

Don't forget to see the outside exhibits and machinery, including a restored section of the old Broughton Flume, which you can learn a bit about on page 54.

Admission:

Adults: $10.00
Children (6 – 12): $6.00
Seniors (60+): $8.00
Students: $8.00
Family Rate (4): $30.00
Military: 10% off
AAA: 10% off

Columbia Gorge Interpretive Center
990 SW Rock Creek Drive
Stevenson, WA 98648
509-427-8211

- Open: Daily – 9:00 a.m. to 5:00 p.m.

 ## Bonneville Dam Fish Viewing Windows

The Bonneville Dam offers visitors the opportunity to see migrating salmon large and small swimming past fish viewing windows on both the Oregon and Washington sides of the dam. This destination is on the Washington side.

Stop in at the Visitor Center to see the salmon making their way upriver, along with interesting exhibits and displays on the fishing techniques and traditions of the Native Americans of the Columbia River Gorge. Note that this event is "fish dependent", so you may want to give the Visitor Center or Fish Count Hotline a call to see if fish are currently running before you stop in. Fish runs in the spring, as well as August through October, peaking in September, provide plenty of fish to see.

Washington Shore Bonneville Dam Visitor Center
Hwy 14 – Milepost 39
Stevenson, WA 98648
541-374-8820

- Open: Daily – 9:00 a.m. to 5:00 p.m.
- Also see the *Average Monthly Fish Count Chart* on page 148 within this book to see if fish may be running during your visit.
- Fish Count Hotline: 541-374-4011

Driving Directions: From the northern end of the Bridge of the Gods at Cascade Locks proceed west for 3.2 miles to Dam Access Road. (1.2 miles *past* the dam / Visitor Center – You don't turn in at the large gate by the Visitor Center) Turn left / south here and follow this *east* 1.2 miles *back* to the dam. Stop at the guard shack and then proceed to the parking area at the Visitor Center entrance.

 ## Fort Cascades National Historic Site

As you pass through this section of the Columbia River Gorge, you may get a sense that it's just a quiet stretch of the river, but it's actually an area rich with history, as explained by the Fort Cascades National Historic Site.

During Lewis and Clark's journey westward, they noted in their journals the existence of a small Native American village here, possibly a seasonal fishing encampment, just downriver from a dangerous set of rapids. In time, pioneers and settlers moved to the area, and as their numbers grew, the small town of Cascades was established in 1850, serving as an outpost for immigrants braving the Oregon Trail, as well as fur traders and others traveling up and down the Columbia. Growing commerce along the river created a need for a means to circumvent the treacherous rapids, and in 1851 work was  completed on a 3-mile stretch of iron-clad wooden rails traversed by mule-drawn carts, known as the Portage Road. By 1855, tensions with the Native Americans had grown, so the U.S. Army seized land near the townsite of Cascades to establish Fort Cascades, a military post which served to protect the road, since it had grown to become an important link in the increasing transportation of goods along the river. In 1863, the Portage Road was replaced by the Cascade Portage Railroad, complete with iron rails and a steam powered locomotive, the counterpart to the Oregon Pony of the Oregon Portage Railroad on the Columbia's southern shore. The completion of the Transcontinental Railroad on the Oregon side of the river, along with the devastating flood of May 19, 1894, led to the demise of the Cascade Portage Railroad and ultimately the entire Cascades townsite.

Stroll along a level 1½ mile loop trail through a shaded forest interspersed with interpretive sites that convey a sense of life in Fort Cascades, as well as the town of Cascades, during this era. See the gravestone of Thomas McNatt, a notable proprietor,  the old roadbed of the Military Portage Road, remnants of the Cascade Portage Railroad, and the sites of the blacksmith's shop, Sutler's Store, McNatt's Barn, the Quartermaster's Complex, and more.

To reach the trailhead, follow the directions for the Bonneville Dam (previous page) but instead of turning off of Hwy 14 onto Dam Access Road and then heading *east* to the dam, turn *west* and follow the signs to the historic site.

 ### Strawberry Loop Hike & Bike Trail

 Here's an interesting trail that offers a number of unique viewpoints of the Columbia River Gorge and Beacon Rock. Running along the perimeter, as well as over the top of Hamilton "Island" is the Strawberry Loop Trail, a 4 mile-long mostly level pathway dotted with a number of benches tucked amongst different species of tall deciduous trees. Make your way to the top and you'll find a collection of 4 benches positioned to take advantage of the 360 degree view of the gorge. Expect to see many different kinds of wildflowers in spots during the summer months, as well as ospreys, eagles, turkey vultures, kestrels, red-tailed hawks and  more, as the path is part of the Great Washington State Birding Trail. Note that the trail starts out as gravel, but soon becomes a somewhat rough pathway mowed into the grass, which you may find difficult for small children to navigate on bikes. The trail's different loops are marked with signage, and restrooms are available at the trailhead.

To reach the trailhead, follow the directions for the Bonneville Dam but instead of turning off of Hwy 14 onto Dam Access Road and heading back *east* to the dam, turn *west* and continue for 1.6 miles until the road ends at the trailhead next to the Columbia River.

 ## Historic Cascade Cemetery

Situated northeast of the town of Bonneville is the historic Cascade Cemetery. Walk the grounds here and you'll get a real sense of the lives of the individuals and families who lived in the area during the mid-1800s to early 1900s, as some of the ornate tombstones convey where folks immigrated from, as well as how they passed.

One of the tombstones you'll find is that of Charles Anton Johnson, who, in addition to working as a foreman on the Columbia River Highway, helped Henry Biddle construct the elaborate trail up the west face of Beacon Rock a few miles west of here from October 1915 to April 1918.

Cascade Cemetery
630 Cascade Drive
Bonneville, WA 98639

To reach the cemetery, follow the directions for the Bonneville Dam but instead of turning *south* off of Hwy 14 onto Dam Access Road, turn *north* at the same point onto Hot Springs Way. Pass under the railroad tracks and in a short distance turn left onto Cascade Drive. You'll find the cemetery on your left.

 Beacon Rock Hike

"*...a remarkable high detached rock Stands in a bottom on the Stard Side near the lower point of this Island on the Stard. Side about 800 feet high and 400 paces round, we call the Beaten Rock.*"

– William Clark, Thursday, October 31, 1805

 Located in the heart of the Columbia River Gorge is Beacon Rock State Park. At 4,456 acres, it is home to a wealth of hiking and biking trails, but its showpiece is the massive Beacon Rock itself. Rising to 848', this former core of a  volcano consists of steep faces of columnar basalt that attract rock climbers and hikers alike. Rising on its west face is a unique nearly mile-long family-friendly trail consisting of over 50 short switchbacks and countless foot bridges all leading to a summit area offering impressive views of the Columbia River Gorge. Though it climbs, the trail is not too steep, and much of it is paved and lined with handrails. As you hike, keep an eye and ear out for rock climbers, such as renowned northwest climber Steve Wolford, who make ascents of the difficult routes on Beacon Rock's vertical south and west faces.

Beacon Rock State Park
34841 Hwy-14
Stevenson, WA 98648

Note: When parking at Beacon Rock, be sure to display a Washington State Discover Pass or a daily parking permit on your dash, *as this lot is patrolled often for permits.* Daily and annual parking permits may be purchased with cash or credit cards at kiosks in the parking lot for $10 and $30 respectively.

Beacon Rock Trail History

In 1915, Henry J. Biddle purchased Beacon Rock from Charles Ladd for $1.00 on the condition that the rock be preserved. In October of that year, Mr. Biddle, with the assistance of Charles Johnson, set out to build a trail to the summit. Constrained by the overhanging features of the north and east faces, and the sheer verticality of the south face, the duo chose to build their trail up the west face, an option that still presented many difficulties. Blasting away rock to create a trail 4' wide, and

spanning open vertical faces with over 20 wooden bridges, they labored in all kinds of weather for two and a half years on the project, finishing in April of 1918, when they opened the new trail and Beacon Rock's summit to the public.

Beacon Rock Café at the Skamania General Store

Seating is *very* limited but the food and service at this small café are excellent. Don't drive by, but instead stop in for breakfast before hiking up to the summit of Beacon Rock, or stop in for lunch afterwards. When you're done eating, visit the General Store next door to pick up some supplies for the rest of the day.

Beacon Rock Café at the Skamania General Store
33001 WA-14
Stevenson, WA 98648
509-427-4825

- Serving Breakfast, Lunch & Dinner

- Open: Wednesday through Monday – 10:00 a.m. to 2:00 p.m. and 4:30 p.m. to 8:30 p.m.

www.Discover-Oregon.com

Cape Horn Overlook – Highway 14

Carved out of a massive cliffside, the Cape Horn Overlook offers visitors one of the most commanding and scenic views found in the Columbia River Gorge as it looks down hundreds of feet upon green pastures, towering fir trees, the broad Columbia River, and Beacon Rock far in the distance.

Note: You'll find the Cape Horn Overlook 9.9 miles west of the Beacon Rock parking area. The overlook doesn't offer much in the way of safe parking as the parking area closely parallels Washington State Highway 14. If parking is sparse when you arrive, keep in mind that there are additional viewing spots a short distance to the east on Highway 14, all of which offer a larger parking area, but a view between the trees.

Cape Horn Hike

Located a short distance east of the Cape Horn Overlook is the trailhead for the popular **Cape Horn Loop Trail**. Gaining 1,500' along its 7.5 mile course, it winds along an upper and lower section of Cape Horn, making its way past expansive viewpoints, a refreshing waterfall, and big leaf maples changing color in the fall. Note that the lower portion of the trail is closed from February 1st to July 15th for nesting Peregrine falcons.

To reach the trailhead, drive 1.4 miles east of the Cape Horn Overlook on Highway 14 and turn north onto Salmon Falls Road. Look for the trailhead parking, complete with restrooms, immediately to your right.

Phone Numbers
Columbia River Gorge – An Explorer's Guide

- Balch Hotel: 541-467-2277
- Biplane Flight – TacAero: 844-359-2827
- Bonneville Dam Interpretive Center: 541-374-8820
- Columbia Gorge Discovery Center: 541-296-8600
- Columbia Gorge Hotel: 541-386-5566
- Columbia Gorge Hotel Spa: 541-387-8451
- Columbia Gorge Interpretive Center: 509-427-8211
- Columbia River Sternwheeler: 503-224-3900
- The Dalles Dam Tour & Visitor Center: 541-296-9778
- Hood River Hotel: 541-386-1900
- Les Schwab Tire Center – Hood River: 541-386-1123
- Les Schwab Tire Center – Goldendale, WA: 509-773-5000
- Les Schwab Tire Center – The Dalles: 541-296-6134
- Lyle Hotel: 509-365-5953
- Nichols Art Glass: 541-296-2143
- Oak Street Hotel: 541-386-3845
- Oregon State Parks Parking Permit: 800-551-6949
- Skamania Lodge: 509-314-4177
- Skamania Lodge Dining Reservations: 509-427-2508
- Skamania Lodge Aerial Park Reservations: 509-427-0202
- Skamania Lodge Zip Line Reservations: 509-427-0202
- The Resort at Skamania Coves: 509-427-4900
- Washington Shore Bonneville Dam Visitor Center: 541-374-8820

www.Discover-Oregon.com

HISTORIC COLUMBIA RIVER GORGE HOTELS

The Columbia River Gorge is rich in history, and what better way to immerse yourself in the essence of that history than staying in a unique historic hotel when making an overnight trip to the gorge? With that in mind, here are some of our favorites...

The 1907 Balch Hotel

Step into the 1907 Balch Hotel and be welcomed with a slower, genuinely friendly pace. Enjoy the freshly baked cookies and refreshingly cool lemonade before checking into your well-appointed period-specific room.

"The Balch" is also a fun weekend destination, with a lot of events occurring here throughout the year. Be sure to sign up for their email newsletter to stay in the know.

If your travel timing works out, we highly recommend you dine at the Balch Hotel upon your arrival. Find a table under the string lights on the patio and enjoy the warm summer evening

as you watch the sun slowly set behind Mt. Hood.

Historic Balch Hotel
40 Heimrich St.
Dufur, OR 97021
541-467-2277

www.BalchHotel.com

The Columbia River Gorge Hotel

Built in 1921 to serve the travelers of the still new Columbia River Highway, The Columbia River Gorge Hotel & Spa today welcomes guests with 40 romantic guestrooms featuring views of the Columbia River or the hotel's tranquil gardens. Guests enjoy contemporary furnishings, including King, Queen, or Double beds, and all rooms feature a private bathroom. In addition, select rooms offer antique canopy beds and a fireplace.

And for those who wish to unwind after a day of traveling, The Spa at The Columbia Gorge Hotel offers the perfect menu of treatments to end your day. Enjoy massages, skin or body treatments, nail and hair services, and more.

The Columbia Gorge Hotel & Spa
4000 Westcliff Drive
Hood River, OR 97031

Hotel Reservations: 541-386-5566
Spa Reservations: 541-387-8451

The Hood River Hotel

The historic and centrally located 1911 Hood River Hotel's rooms and suites welcome guests with luxurious accommodations, including European style linens, fluffy pillows and down duvets, eco-friendly spa-quality bath products, Wi-Fi, flat screen TVs, and views of the city or Columbia River.

Being in the heart of "old town" Hood River, you'll be close to all kinds of cafes, coffee shops, wineries, and brew pubs. In addition, you can dine at a nearby eatery, or enjoy a meal at Broder Ost, the hotel's European inspired restaurant, before relaxing and enjoying a glass of wine in front of the wood burning fireplace in the lobby. *Hood River Hotel Photo © Ian Poellet*

Hood River Hotel
102 SW Oak Street
Hood River, OR 97031
541-386-1900

Old Parkdale Inn Bed & Breakfast

Choose to stay at the Old Parkdale Inn Bed & Breakfast and you'll be treated to the warm hospitality of the owners, Steve and Mary Pellegrini. Located at the halfway point of the Mt. Hood Scenic Byway, which takes you up and around Mt. Hood, and "this close" to Mt. Hood itself, this 1910 Craftsman home welcomes guests with three quaint rooms, each offering queen beds, luxurious beddings, flat screen TVs, private baths, free Wi-Fi and more. Better yet, right outside your door is the Hood River Fruit Loop, which you can spend all day exploring after enjoying a delicious breakfast featuring fresh fruits from the Hood River Valley.

Old Parkdale Inn Bed & Breakfast
4932 Baseline Drive
Parkdale, OR 97041
541-352-5551

Note that the inn features an Electric Vehicle Charging Station.

Oak Street Hotel

The historic Oak Street Hotel reaches back to 1909, when it was built as a home in the early days of Hood River, before the completion of the Columbia River Highway. Beautifully restored, this award-winning hotel welcomes guests with small rooms filled  with character, as well as refined amenities. Hand-forged iron queen beds, hand-crafted furniture, specially formulated bath products and more all await guests after a day of exploration. Note that while all rooms have en-suite bathrooms, some rooms have a bath separated only by a plush drapery curtain, so be sure to inquire if you wish to have more privacy during your stay.

> Oak Street Hotel
> 610 Oak Street
> Hood River, OR 97031
> 541-386-3845

Victor Trevitt Guest House

Built in 1868 and recently restored with impeccable period-specific detail and antique furnishings, the historic Victor Trevitt Guest House makes for a perfect taste of days gone past in The Dalles.

> Victor Trevitt Guest House
> 214 W 4th Street
> The Dalles, OR
> 541-980-3522

Born in 1827, Victor Trevitt moved to The Dalles in 1853, and as a printer, entrepreneur, businessman, state legislator and the first judge to preside at the small Wasco County Courthouse, he played an important role in shaping the growth of this area and developing The Dalles.

The 1905 Lyle Hotel

Like much of the west, the railroads played an important role in the history of the Columbia River Gorge. Wood, wheat, grain, wool and other materials relied on the Spokane, Portland & Seattle (SP&S) Railway to move goods shortly after the turn of the prior century, and the folks who used that railway relied upon The Lyle Hotel for a place to dine and rest.

Today, the historic Lyle Hotel welcomes travelers from around the Northwest and the world with luxurious accommodations, period-specific rooms, fine dining, and warm hospitality. You'll find all 10 of the private guestrooms on the 2nd floor, with five shared, yet still private, restrooms and baths across the hall. And for those who prefer not to hear the sound of history from the railroad tracks nearby...you'll also find a set of earplugs.

The Lyle Hotel
100 Seventh Street
Lyle, WA 98635
509-365-5953

Skamania Lodge

With its large timbers, warm wood paneling, Mission-style furnishings, hand-crafted stonework, and black wrought iron accents, Skamania Lodge is reminiscent of the historic grand lodges of America's National Parks. Guests may relax with a book in front of the three-story stone fireplace, watch the evening fade from the great lawn while taking in the sweeping view of the Columbia River, or enjoy the heated pool, the dry sauna, or indoor and outdoor whirlpools. And for true indulgence, relax after a day of exploring with a visit to the full-service Waterleaf spa. Seeking more adventure? Then enjoy the Skamania Lodge's lofty new zip line or aerial park, or take one of the three short hikes around the 18-hole par 70 golf course located amidst towering firs and a couple of large mountain ponds, complete with basking turtles.

Retire for the evening in one of Skamania Lodge's 254 nicely appointed rooms, each of which reflect the grand essence of the lodge, or opt to stay in one of the "Away in the Woods" Tree Houses. Set up off the ground in the forest, each sleeps up to four guests and offers a wealth of modern amenities.

Photos courtesy of Skamania Lodge

Skamania Lodge
1131 SW Skamania Lodge Way
Stevenson, WA 98648
844-432-4748

Historic Government Mineral Springs Guard Station

Situated at the base of a dozen towering old growth firs in the Gifford Pinchot National Forest is the historic Government Mineral Springs Guard Station. Built by the Civilian Conservation Corps in 1937 and restored in 2002, this remote cabin offers travelers "rustic charm", privacy, and an opportunity to disconnect. Guests will find no running water or electricity, so don't plan on charging your phone and checking email. Instead, enjoy a book by a crackling fire and the light of the gas lamps after exploring the nearby old growth forest that is steep in history, as the area used to be home to a hotel, bath houses, a dance pavilion, store and gardens over 100 years ago.

Inside, guests will find a kitchen with a propane stove, gas heat, a dining area with a kitchen table, a living room with two futon couches, two bedrooms upstairs, one of which includes bunk beds, two twin beds and a nearby outhouse. (Remember, there's no running water. Think of it as camping in a cabin.) The cabin is open year-round and is very popular in the summer. As a result, it is best to make reservations early, up to 6 months in advance. Reservations may be made online at www.Recreation.gov or by calling 877-444-6777.

Government Mineral Springs Guard Station
2455 Hwy 141
Trout Lake, WA 98650
Ranger Station: 509-395-3400

WANT TO VISIT MT. HOOD AND TIMBERLINE LODGE?

If you've never visited Mt. Hood and Timberline Lodge, but you've always wanted to, then making a trip "up to the mountain" while visiting the gorge may be just the ticket ...since you're in the neighborhood.

One of Oregon's most famous icons, historic Timberline Lodge, set at the 6,000' timberline of Mt. Hood, welcomes visitors with a commanding presence in a lofty alpine setting, with snowy 11,245' Mt. Hood towering above to the north while the summits of the Oregon Cascades stretch far to the south. Guests are welcomed with classic 1930s-era mountain lodge architecture featuring hand-sculpted stonework, a board and batten exterior, and a massive wood beam interior featuring 70 guest rooms and showcasing a six-sided stone fireplace reaching 92' high.

Be sure to allow time to visit the museum dedicated to the construction of the lodge, which is located on the first floor, as well as to sit for a spell by the fireplace to get a sense of the ambiance and history of the building. A gift shop offering Timberline Lodge related gifts and locally made products is also located on the second floor.

Timberline Lodge
27500 W Leg Rd.
Timberline Lodge, OR 97028

Driving Directions from Exit 64 in Hood River:

While traveling on I-84, take *Exit 64 – Mt. Hood HWY – Govt. Camp.* At the stop, turn right and follow this for 0.2 miles as the road makes a sweeping leftward curve to a 4-way stop. Proceed straight at the 4-way stop, which will put you onto Highway 35 southbound. Follow Highway 35 for 38.2 miles and then merge onto Highway 26 heading west. Continue on Highway 26 westbound for 2.4 miles to Timberline Highway, which is a two lane road. Turn right onto Timberline Highway and follow this for 5.5 miles as it climbs to Timberline Lodge. If you have reservations at the lodge, then you may park in the upper parking area, close to the lodge's entrance. If not, then you must park in the larger lot below and walk up to the lodge.

THE HISTORIC COLUMBIA RIVER HIGHWAY

Many of those who explore the Gorge do so by traveling the "King of Roads", the Historic Columbia River Highway.

Built by eccentric railroad lawyer and entrepreneur Sam Hill and engineer Samuel Lancaster from 1913 to 1922, and modeled after Switzerland's Axenstrasse roadway around Lake Lucerne, the Historic Columbia River Highway stretches for nearly 75 miles from Troutdale to The Dalles, passing amidst the green maples, brightly colored moss and lush ferns of the Columbia River Gorge's western end before transitioning to the Ponderosa Pines and small oak trees dotting the semi-arid plateaus and hillsides of its eastern end. Along the way, this "great scenic boulevard", built for the Model Ts of its era, reveals a road that is an artistic masterpiece, showcasing retaining walls, guard rails, and structures master crafted from hand-hewn stone, logs and timbers. Connecting it all is a collection of graceful bridges which allow travelers to continue on their journey past stunning vistas and majestic waterfalls, with names like Latourell, Wahkeena, and Oneonta, as they make their way around, down, over and even through towering basalt cliffs toward their destination.

Though initially dedicated in 1916, the road began to pass into another era when construction on the I-84 freeway began in the 1930s. To make room for the new freeway, portions of the now "old" Columbia River Highway were blasted away, and tunnels through the basalt cliffs were either filled in or demolished. Today, however, portions of the Columbia River Highway are being reclaimed and restored. The Mosier Tunnels have been cleared of fill and are now open to cyclists and pedestrians, cyclists can ride from Troutdale to Cascade Locks, and the final segments of the Historic Columbia River Highway State Trail are being finished, thus allowing travelers to soon traverse from Troutdale all the way to The Dalles on the old highway or on newly restored portions, with much of the journey closed to cars.

To learn more about Sam Hill, Samuel Lancaster, and the construction of the Historic Columbia River Highway, we highly recommend the book *Building the Columbia River Highway - They Said It Couldn't Be Done* by Peg Willis. You may want to pick up a copy and read it as you begin to explore the Gorge. You'll be glad you did!

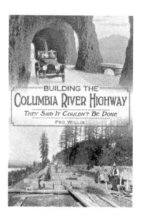

US Army Corps of Engineers ®
Portland District

AVERAGE MONTHLY FISH COUNT AT BONNEVILLE DAM

Here are the average monthly fish counts of common adult fish that pass Bonneville Lock and Dam. These fish are unique because they are anadromous (they begin their lives in fresh water, spend part of their life in the ocean, and return to fresh water to spawn). The majority of fish migrating upstream past Bonneville do so between March and November each year. The following numbers represent the ten year monthly average from 2006-2015.

Month	CHINOOK* SALMON (KING)	SOCKEYE SALMON (BLUEBACK)	COHO* SALMON (SILVER)	STEELHEAD TROUT	SHAD	LAMPREY
January	1	0	0	543	0	0
February	3	0	0	387	0	0
March	363	0	0	1,479	0	0
April	54,569	0	0	1,361	0	0
May	116,352	84	0	1,727	240,876	787
June	79,770	193,212	0	9,502	1,907,935	5,133
July	37,564	91,374	2	87,796	113,624	10,706
August	111,089	442	10,266	154,124	272	4,386
September	429,914	13	71,599	76,994	0	1,190
October	43,332	0	46,645	10,874	0	64
November	2,117	0	5,466	1,937	0	19
December	53	0	183	779	0	1

* Jacks included

Fish climbing the fish ladder can either jump over the walls that separate pools in the ladders, or swim through holes in the walls.

ROAD TRIP THE
COLUMBIA RIVER GORGE

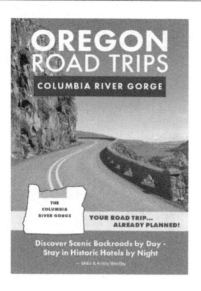

Oregon Road Trips –
Columbia River Gorge Edition

Journey along the Historic Columbia River Highway deep into the Columbia River Gorge, where you'll spend 3 to 5 days seeing the Gorge's majestic waterfalls, flying in a vintage 2-seater biplane, hiking through the historic Mosier Tunnels, stepping into the void on an exciting zip line tour, walking amidst the Gorge's beautiful spring wildflowers, finding your next book at Oregon's oldest bookstore, and even spotting Giraffes, Zebras, Camels, Bison and more!

Your Columbia River Gorge road trip awaits, and it's already planned for you!

Available Now at Retailers Throughout Oregon, Discover-Oregon.com and Online

ROAD TRIP OREGON'S MAJESTIC MT. HOOD

Oregon Road Trips – Mt. Hood Edition

An alpine Oregon Road Trip adventure is waiting for you!

Set out on an exciting Oregon road trip where every night ends at a charming historic hotel, finishing with majestic Timberline Lodge at 6,000' on the south shoulder of Mt. Hood! Explore the Historic Columbia River Highway, hike the unique Mosier Tunnels route, visit Oregon's oldest bookstore, walk among the Columbia River Gorge's colorful spring wildflowers, fly in a vintage 2-seater biplane, ride to over 7,000' on the Magic Mile Chairlift, discover the rustic and remote 1889 Cloud Cap Inn on Mt. Hood's eastern flank, and so much more.

Available Now at Retailers Throughout Oregon, Discover-Oregon.com and Online

NOW ENJOY AN
OREGON COAST ROAD TRIP

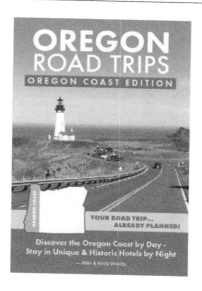

Oregon Road Trips – Oregon Coast Edition

If you enjoy exploring the Columbia River Gorge, then you'll really enjoy exploring all of the grandeur of Oregon's dramatic coastline during an adventurous 9-day road trip from Astoria south to Brookings. You'll journey along Oregon's beautiful Highway 101 as you discover countless scenic beaches, tour historic lighthouses, wander through quaint beach towns, watch whales spouting just off shore, ride in the cab of a 1925 steam locomotive, eat tasty Dungeness Crab fresh off the boat...or catch your own, stay in historic hotels, explore unique shops, meet friendly people and so much more!

Your perfect 9-day Oregon Coast road trip awaits and it's already planned for you, from start to finish!

Available Now at Retailers Throughout Oregon, Discover-Oregon.com and Online

A NORTHEAST OREGON ROAD TRIP

Oregon Road Trips – Northeast Edition

Now discover Northeast Oregon's scenic backroads and byways by day, *while staying in historic hotels by night!*

With our *Oregon Road Trips – Northeast Edition* guide, you'll explore the scenic beauty of Northeast Oregon while you ride aboard a historic steam train, wander Oregon ghost towns, ascend in a cable tram to over 8,000', stay at the 1907 Balch Hotel, board the Sumpter Valley Dredge, explore Cottonwood Canyon, ride the rails on a 2-seater, explore unique shops, eat at great restaurants, meet friendly people and so much more!

An adventurous Northeast Oregon road trip awaits, and it's already planned for you!

Available Now at Retailers Throughout Oregon, Discover-Oregon.com and Online

AN EXCITING SE OREGON ROAD TRIP AWAITS

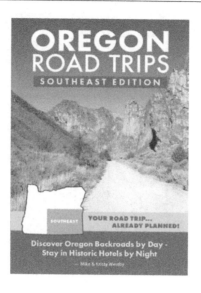

Oregon Road Trips – Southeast Edition

Ready for a remote Oregon adventure? Then you'll love *Oregon Road Trips – Southeast Edition*. As with all of our road trip guides, you'll simply turn each page as you motor along and choose which points of interest to stop at and explore during your day's journey, *all while making your way toward that evening's lodging in a historic Oregon hotel.*

You'll drive to the top of 9,734' Steens Mountain, stay in the 1923 Frenchglen Hotel, explore the remote Leslie Gulch, see how stage coaches are built, dig for fossils, hike "Crack in the Ground", look for wild Mustangs, eat at a truly unique and remote Oregon restaurant, marvel at the geologic wonders of the Journey Through Time Scenic Byway, and so much more!

Available Now at Retailers Throughout Oregon, Discover-Oregon.com and Online

EXPLORE
SOUTHWEST OREGON

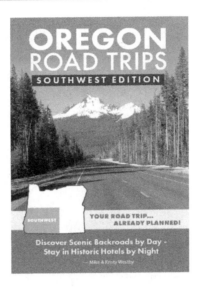

Oregon Road Trips – Southwest Edition

Another Oregon adventure is already planned out for you!

Visit 13 historic covered bridges, spend a night in Crater Lake Lodge, discover a vintage aircraft museum, enjoy a play in Ashland, explore deep into the Oregon Caves, wander an Oregon ghost town, see some of Oregon's most beautiful waterfalls, tour the Applegate Wine Trail, and so much more on your 9-day road trip through Southwest Oregon. As with our other Oregon Road Trip books, you'll simply motor along while you discover Oregon...*and finish each night at a unique historic hotel!*

Available Now at Retailers Throughout Oregon, Discover-Oregon.com and Online

DISCOVER
CENTRAL OREGON

Central Oregon is a big place. To the west, high Cascade lakes and snowy peaks offer a world of alpine adventure, while to the east, the high desert beckons travelers to another world, one filled with thrilling experiences and geological wonders. In between is a land of scenic vistas, majestic waterfalls, amazing attractions, and countless outdoor and indoor adventures just waiting to be explored, and they're all here for you in the new *Central Oregon – An Explorer's Guide!* Use this guide to discover over 150 unique attractions, destinations, and experiences where you'll discover nine thundering waterfalls, set out on a moonlight kayaking adventure, walk among WWII era aircraft, hike through Oregon's high desert, ride a summer chairlift up Mt. Bachelor to enjoy some amazing alpine views, drive to the top of Paulina Peak, watch world-class rock climbing up close, paddleboard and kayak on the slow flowing Deschutes River, explore an ancient lava tube, and much more!

Available Now at Retailers Throughout Oregon, Discover-Oregon.com and Online

WHAT TO SEE, DO & EXPLORE ON THE OREGON COAST

At 363 miles long, Oregon's scenic coastline is filled with countless natural wonders and attractions to see, do, and explore. Hike to a high bluff to watch for whales, walk a long sandy beach, explore a historic lighthouse, catch a live Dungeness crab, join in the fun of a sandcastle building contest, even ride aboard an old-fashioned steam train. The problem is...how do you uncover all of these activities to get the most out of your trip? The solution is the new *Oregon Coast Guide.* Inside these pages, you'll discover over 200 fun and adventurous things to see, do and explore while visiting the Oregon Coast, complete with descriptions, photos, maps, tips, a whale watching guide and much more.

Available Now at Retailers Throughout Oregon, Discover-Oregon.com and Online

DISCOVER
WASHINGTON'S
OLYMPIC PENINSULA

Washington's Olympic Peninsula has always been somewhat of a mystery, but now it's an adventurous and perfectly planned 6-day road trip! Set out to discover this exciting world that varies from high alpine peaks and lofty hiking trails to long sandy beaches and captivating ocean vistas. Stay at and explore the busy Victorian seaport of Port Townsend, visit a historic lighthouse, tour a vintage airplane museum, kayak on the Strait of Juan de Fuca, see majestic Orcas, Humpbacks, and Gray Whales, sleep in your very own castle, stand in the quietest place in the United States, explore unique shops, eat at great restaurants, meet friendly people, and so much more!

Your perfect Northern Olympic Peninsula road trip awaits...and it's already planned for you!

Available Now at Retailers
Throughout Washington and Online

EXPLORE WASHINGTON'S OLYMPIC PENINSULA

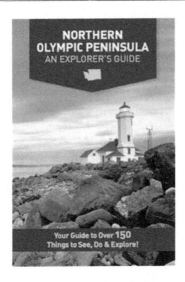

Now easily discover over 150 things to see, do and explore on Washington's Northern Olympic Peninsula!

The majestic northern Olympic Peninsula is filled with scenic vistas, beautiful beaches, graceful waterfalls, amazing attractions, and countless adventures, and they're all waiting for you in the *Northern Olympic Peninsula – An Explorer's Guide.* Tour a vintage aeroplane museum, visit historic lighthouses, learn how wooden kayaks are made, sleep in your very own castle, see Orcas, Gray Whales, and Humpbacks up close, discover the most beautiful waterfall on the Olympic Peninsula, explore historic Fort Worden, hike stunning Shi Shi and Rialto beaches, hike the captivating Hoh Rainforest, wander old town Port Townsend, and so much more!

Available Now at Retailers
Throughout Washington and Online

OREGON & 1

Oregon, we want to start a grass roots movement.

Imagine if every business in Oregon, large or small, huge or tiny, promoted *at least* one other Oregon business...at no charge, which is completely unrelated to their business.

- A small café promotes a bookstore on its menu.

- A bookstore promotes a historical carousel with a placard by the cash register.

- A historical carousel promotes a tour provider with a small sign near the ticket counter.

- A tour provider promotes a tire store with a mention on its brochures.

- A tire store promotes a local hotel with a note on its invoices.

- A local hotel promotes a theater in the next town over with current showtimes listed at its check-in counter.

- A local theater promotes an auto repair shop with a small sign on its door.

- An auto repair shop promotes a small café with a menu placed in the waiting room.

Creative opportunities to promote Oregon businesses are endless. Better yet, each requires *very little effort or expense* and can start right now...at your business. How do you decide who to promote? Let your employees pick their favorites and rotate their choices on a regular basis.

With all of us extending a hand to our fellow Oregonians beginning today, we can build a powerful interconnected web that reaches all across the state and cross-promotes thousands and thousands of Oregon businesses every day, thus lifting our state's economy, adding to your neighbor's paycheck, and bringing more business to your business.

Oregon and 1!

WE RECOMMEND OREGON & WASHINGTON AUTHORS & SMALL BUSINESSES...

Building The Columbia River Highway

The intriguing story of how visionary artists, poets and engineers came together to forge a route through the mighty Columbia River Gorge and create the nation's first scenic highway, a "poem in stone." Ride along with author Peg Willis as she explores the beginnings of this miracle highway, the men who created it, and the obstacles they overcame on the road to its completion.

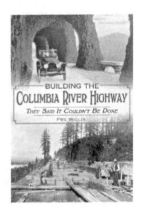

Twila's English Toffee

Hand crafted in the Columbia River Gorge using only high-quality ingredients, Twila's English Toffee is a crisp, buttery and savory delight you'll want to enjoy every time you make a trip to the Gorge. Pick up a package at a local Gorge specialty retailer, or order a package or two or three as a gift for family and friends at www.TwilasToffee.com.

Les Schwab Tire Centers

If you're on the road and have a flat tire, brake issues or a similar problem, we highly recommend the very helpful folks at your nearby Les Schwab Tire Center. You'll find locations in Hood River, OR, The Dalles, OR, and Goldendale, WA. Their phone numbers are listed on page 136.

Antiques & Oddities

A popular Columbia River Gorge "antiques destination" for over 20 years, Antiques & Oddities in Bingen, WA is home to an eclectic collection of quality antiques from near and far, including Asia and Europe. Stop in when you're in the Gorge, and be sure to make your way downstairs to check out their latest arrivals.

Antiques & Oddities
211 W. Steuben St., Bingen, WA 98605
509-493-4242

Mt. Hood – Adventures of the Wy'East Climbers

A fascinating read about the intrepid climbers of the Golden Era on Mt. Hood, the 1930s. Learn all about those who dared to forge first ascents, battled the elements to rescue fellow climbers, and manned the lookout atop Mt. Hood's lofty and often violent summit. Available online, as well as at the Mt. Hood Cultural Center & Museum in Government Camp.

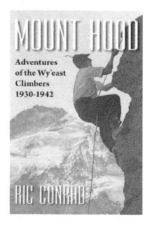

MOUNT HOOD
Adventures
of the Wy'east
Climbers
1930-1942

RIC CONRAD

75 Classic Rides: Oregon

From an after-work ride through Portland's neighborhood streets or a family cycle along the flat Willamette Valley Scenic Bikeway, to a multi-day tour in the salty breezes of the Oregon coast— if you're seeking the best bike trails in Oregon, you'll find plenty to ride in Jim Moore's *75 Classic Rides: Oregon.*

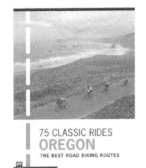

Are You a Disneyland Fan?

Enjoy a fascinating and entertaining book which reveals over 250 of the fun hidden secrets and story elements that the Disney Imagineers have purposely hidden for Disneyland guests to find and enjoy, complete with 225 photos!

Available online, as well as at the prestigious Walt Disney Family Museum, the Walt Disney Boyhood Home, and the Walt Disney Hometown Museum.

Want Even More Disneyland Secrets?

Discover the in-depth stories behind 50 magical story elements of Disneyland, *many of which are published here for the very first time.* Compiled from extensive research and lengthy interviews with Disney Legends, Imagineers, and other Disney notables.

Available online, as well as at the prestigious Walt Disney Family Museum, the Walt Disney Boyhood Home, and the Walt Disney Hometown Museum.

Are You a Walt Disney World Fan?

See and experience Walt Disney World in an entirely new way! Written by Oregon author Mike Fox, *The Hidden Secrets & Stories of Walt Disney World* reveals over 500 of the fun secret story elements that the Disney Imagineers have hidden throughout all four parks, complete with more than 400 photos.

Available online, as well as at the Walt Disney Hometown Museum and the Walt Disney Boyhood Home.

Camp Attitude

"Changing lives one camper at a time!"

Camp Attitude provides a welcoming camp experience for disabled youth and their families. Here, children with special needs can participate in all of the fun, games, excitement and interaction of a thrilling week-long "summer camp" experience, all for a nominal fee, thanks to donations from contributors who enjoy seeing a smile on a child's face...and a squirt gun in their hand!

Camp Attitude is a faith-based non-profit organization, and donations may be made by visiting their web site at www.CampAttitude.org

Camp Attitude
PO Box 2017
45829 S Santiam Hwy
Foster, OR 97345
541-401-1052

Are You Looking to Explore Bend, Oregon?

If your explorations take you to Bend, Oregon and you'd like to rent a nice home while you're there, we'd like to recommend you consider our place. It sleeps six, is nicely furnished, and is centrally located to all kinds of fun and adventurous year-round activities. Better yet, if you contact us directly, you save having to pay the "service fees" you find when you rent a place online.

If you'd like information about our home, feel free to send Mike a note at ContactUS@Discover-Oregon.com.

NOTES

Made in the USA
Las Vegas, NV
17 February 2021